Jan Bondeson is a retired senior lecturer and consultant physician at Cardiff University, and a distinguished true crime author; his previous critically acclaimed books include *The London Monster*, *Murder Houses of London*, *Rivals of the Ripper* and *Victorian Murders*.

DOCTOR POISON

The Extraordinary Career of Dr George Henry Lamson, Victorian Murderer Par Excellence

Jan Bondeson

Copyright © 2021 Jan Bondeson

The moral right of the author has been asserted.

Apart from any fair dealing for the purposes of research or private study, or criticism or review, as permitted under the Copyright, Designs and Patents Act 1988, this publication may only be reproduced, stored or transmitted, in any form or by any means, with the prior permission in writing of the publishers, or in the case of reprographic reproduction in accordance with the terms of licences issued by the Copyright Licensing Agency. Enquiries concerning reproduction outside those terms should be sent to the publishers.

Matador
9 Priory Business Park,
Wistow Road, Kibworth Beauchamp,
Leicestershire. LE8 0RX
Tel: 0116 279 2299
Email: books@troubador.co.uk
Web: www.troubador.co.uk/matador
Twitter: @matadorbooks

ISBN 978 1800465 145

British Library Cataloguing in Publication Data.
A catalogue record for this book is available from the British Library.

Typeset in 10.5pt Aldine401 BT by Troubador Publishing Ltd, Leicester, UK

Matador is an imprint of Troubador Publishing Ltd

CONTENTS

	PREFACE	vii
I.	THE FAMILY AND EARLY CAREER OF GEORGE HENRY LAMSON	1
II.	AMERICA AND WARTIME SERVICE	14
III.	ROTHERFIELD AND BOURNEMOUTH	29
IV.	AMERICA, SHANKLIN AND LONDON	44
V.	THE HOUR OF DEATH	63
VI.	DR LAMSON AT BAY	77
VII.	DR LAMSON AT BOW STREET	95
VIII.	THE TRIAL OF GEORGE HENRY LAMSON	111
IX.	RESPITE AND AFFIDAVITS	136
X.	THE END	161
XI.	SOME REMAINING MYSTERIES	174
XII.	THE CURSE OF THE LAMSONS	188
XIII.	SUCH DEADLY DOCTORS	201
XIV	CONCLUDING REMARKS	235
	FOOTNOTES	238

PREFACE

In April 2001, my mother came from Sweden to visit me, and since I had recently moved from a flat in London to a large house in South Wales, I was able to present her with a good deal of entertainment. Since she had a strong fondness for historical monuments, we drove to see the castles of Caerphilly, Chepstow, Raglan, Kidwelly and Carreg Cennen. One day, we went for an expedition to Hay-on-Wye, the world-famous Town of Books, travelling on the old mountain road from Llanwihangel Crucorney via Capel-y-ffin, stopping at ancient Llanthony Abbey on the way. This old road was not much used, and coming through a bend in my TVR sports car, I was dismayed to see a large yellow dog sleeping peacefully on the tarmac just in front of us! When I braked hard and sounded the horn, the Welsh cur took a leap to safety, barking angrily at being disturbed in his slumber.

After admiring the glorious mountain views and descending on the other side of the summit, we arrived safely in Hay-on-Wye. Being a vigorous book collector, I lost no time before searching some of the bookshops, and just before luncheon, I found a copy of Hargrave Lee Adam's *Trial of George Henry Lamson*. Although the book was in an unattractive library binding, ex Berkshire County Libraries HQ Reserve Stock, I purchased it since it cost just £2.95, and since it was one of my ambitions in life to accumulate a complete set of the Notable British Trials, all 83 volumes of them. During luncheon, I read some of Mr Adam's introduction, finding it most hilarious that the murderous doctor had greeted his victim with the ludicrous words "Why, how fat you are looking, Percy, old boy!" before going on to entice the hapless lad to his death by exclaiming "Here, Percy, you are a swell pill-taker; take this, and show Mr Bedbrook how easily it may be swallowed!"

For many years to come, Hargrave Lee Adam's *Trial of George Henry Lamson* stood among my other Notable British Trials, unconsulted after the initial reading back in 2001. I eventually managed to complete my collection of these agreeable books, but by that time I no longer had a mother, since she had died at an advanced age in 2009. In 2014, I decided to complete a project that had been ongoing since 2010, namely to compile two books based on a collection of old images from the *Illustrated Police News* and other Victorian periodicals, held by an old man in Cardiff whom I had befriended: one book (*Strange Victoriana*; Amberley Publishing 2016) about Forteana and strange events, the other (*Victorian Murders*; Amberley Publishing 2017) about Victorian murder stories. One of the cases covered in the second book was that of the celebrated medical miscreant Dr George Henry Lamson, and while making some researches, I was astounded to see how much new material came to light with regard to Lamson's previous life, his motive, and the completion of his heinous deeds. When I discussed this book with my old friend, the late Richard Whittington-Egan, he asked whether I had been able to unearth important new evidence in any of the cases included. My response was that although I had been able to shed some much-needed new light on the unsolved murders of Mrs Ann Reville in Slough and Mrs Sarah Dinah Noel in Ramsgate, the case of Dr Lamson stood out with regard to the amount of novel information being accumulated. He then said that a short book on the Lamson case would not come amiss, and the very same evening, I added it to my list of potential book projects.[1] After three years of research and writing, it has passed from the nebulous world of purported book projects to the solid wooden shelf of published books waiting to be sold; I wish it many readers.

I.

THE FAMILY AND EARLY CAREER OF GEORGE HENRY LAMSON

William Lamson, the earliest ancestor of the Lamson family in the United States, emigrated from England to America in 1634, and became a freeman and farmer in Ipswich, Massachusetts. He was a man of some standing in the local community, and was elected supervisor of the swine and cattle let out on the common; he had authority to seize stray animals and impound them until their owner had paid a fine. He was also elected inspector of fences and permitted to fell 300 trees to make some improvements to the enclosures. He was part of the local militia, trained to protect the settlement and fight hostile Indian tribes. William Lamson married Sarah Ayers, fathering four sons and four daughters. He died in 1658 or 1659. His eldest son John Lamson, born in 1642, also became a prosperous farmer in Ipswich. He married Martha Perkins and fathered many children, seven of whom reached adulthood. In his will, he partitioned a considerable estate among his four sons and three surviving daughters. Since he could not read or write, he made his mark on the will in lieu of a proper signature.

William Lamson, the eldest son of John Lamson, was born in 1675. He took over the Lamson farm in Ipswich, his homestead being next to that of his brother, Ensign Samuel Lamson. A prosperous farmer, he allowed his sons Benjamin, Thomas and

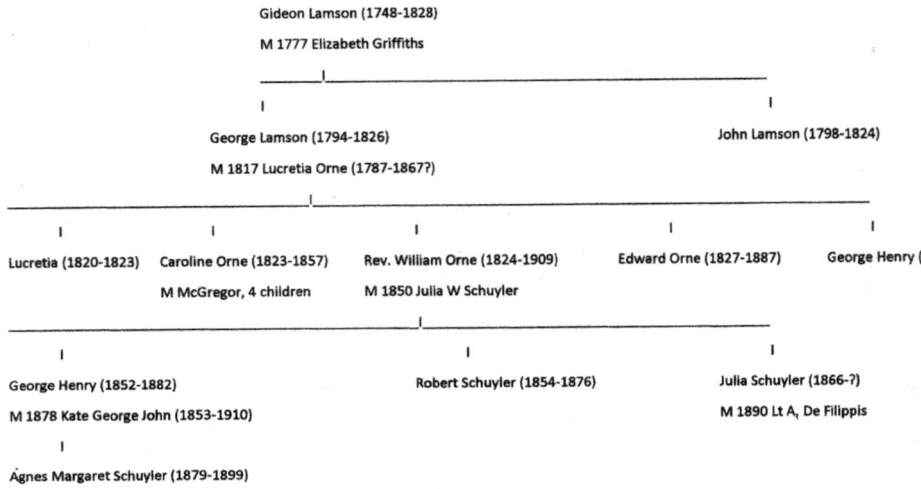

1. The Lamson pedigree.

Jonathan to build houses of their own on his land. His eldest son William, born in 1708, had left Ipswich as a young man, to become a tailor in Exeter, New Hampshire. He married Joanna Tuttle and had three sons and two daughters. The second son Gideon Lamson, born in 1748, also lived in Exeter, being something of a jack of all trades, working as a tailor, a merchant, and a trader. He was well thought of locally, and was made a Selectman of Exeter in 1786, and a Coroner of Rockingham County in 1790. He had two sons, both of whom he survived: George, born in 1794 and John, born in 1798 and dead in 1824. George Lamson had a more distinguished career than any of his forebears. A graduate of Bowdoin College, he afterwards studied law, with considerable success. In 1817, George married Lucretia Bourne Orne, who may well have come from a wealthy family; in 1823, they moved to New York City, where he set up practice as a lawyer.

George and Lucretia Lamson had five children: the daughter Lucretia who died young, the daughter Caroline Orne, born in 1823, the son William Orne, born in 1824, the son Edward Orne, born in 1827, and the son George Henry, whose year of birth is not recorded. It must have been quite a blow to this large family when George Lamson died unexpectedly in 1826, at the age of just 32. His widow Lucretia looked after the four surviving children as well as she could, and remained in New York City, being recorded to be living at No. 31 Fourth Street in 1841. The daughter Caroline Orne married a man named McGregor and had four children of her own. The son Edward Orne married but did not have issue. The son George Henry lived in China for a while and knew Napoleon III of France; he died in New York City in 1857, unmarried and without issue.[1]

★

The son William Orne Lamson, grandson of Gideon Lamson and a member of the seventh generation of Lamsons in the United States, shared his father's talent for an academic education. He studied at New York University, where he was a member of the Psi Upsilon Fraternity. He graduated as a Bachelor of Arts in 1849 and as a Master of Arts in 1852. In March 1851, he was ordained to the deaconate, and in December 1852 to the priesthood, by Bishop Chase. In August 1851, he became Rector of St John's Church in Stockport, New York, and in April 1852, Rector of the Church of the Ascension, South Brooklyn.

In 1850, William Orne Lamson married Julia Wood Schuyler, the daughter of the wealthy New York 'railroad king' and financier Robert Schuyler, and granddaughter of US Representative Philip Jeremiah Schuyler. It was clearly a very favourable marriage for the Rev. Mr Lamson, whose family would not be troubled by any financial worries for many years to come. They soon had two sons: George Henry, born on September 8 1852, and Robert Schuyler, born in 1854. The Rev. Mr Lamson took his work seriously, and he appears to have been a good clergyman, who had

2. The Rev. William Orne Lamson.

genuine religious feelings and a prominent sense of philanthropy, and who stayed away from telling untruths, embezzling money and molesting children. He was on the lookout for more stimulating work than what was offered by his suburban flock in New York, and had success in early 1858, when he was selected by Bishop Williams of Connecticut to take charge of the American Episcopal Church in Paris. On June 26 1858, the Rev. Mr Lamson left New York City on the steamship *Arago*, bound for Southampton and Le Havre, bringing with him his wife and his two young sons. On August 16 1858, the *Morning Chronicle* could report that "The Rev. Wm. O. Lamson, of New York, has arrived in Paris, for the purpose of establishing the service of the American Episcopal Church in the French capital, and will officiate to-morrow in the Chapelle Taitbout."[2]

The Rev. Mr Lamson settled down in Paris with his family. The state of the American Episcopal Church in the French capital was not a particularly healthy one, as it would turn out: the congregation had access to the American Chapel in the Rue de Berri, but it had to be shared with other Christian persuasions catering to American expatriates. There was a good deal of idle hands and intriguing minds among the American men of religion in Paris, and not all of them appreciated the Rev. Mr Lamson coming to reinforce the Episcopal Church. After Mr Lamson had insisted that a full Sunday Episcopal service should be held at the American Chapel, his enemies referred to him as "a missionary of disturbance" and in other terms of disrespect. It was rumoured that the Episcopal bishops in Connecticut, New Jersey and New York had sent Lamson on a mission to break up the union at the American Chapel, and strengthen the American Episcopalists in Paris by constructing a church of their own. But although his enemies wrote some poison-pen letters to the religious magazines back in America, and plotted to have the Rev. Mr Lamson sent back to New York, Lamson's position was secure, since the Episcopalists gathered behind him. They appreciated his efforts to strengthen the position of their congregation, and get them a church of their own. Furthermore, he had the support of the powerful American Episcopal bishops who had sent him off on his mission to Paris.[3]

The Rev. Mr Lamson moved into an apartment at No. 19 Rue Castellane with his family. His two sons George Henry and Robert Schuyler both went to a French school, where they became perfectly bilingual. George Henry in particular showed early promise as a scholar, and the Rev. Mr Lamson had hopes that he would enjoy a successful academic career. Mrs Julia Lamson also took a vigorous part in church life, becoming the organist of the Episcopal congregation. Since the Rev. Mr Lamson found it unsatisfactory that his flock had to worship at various shared churches and chapels, he made exertions to have a new American Church constructed. But although there was no shortage of wealthy Americans in Paris, the cultural capital of Europe during the second Empire, and although quite a few French noblemen had married American heiresses, money was lacking for such an expensive project. The Rev. Mr Lamson went back to the United States in 1861, 1862 and 1863, to negotiate with the Episcopal bishops and drum up financial support from wealthy people back home, and in the end he had success. Land was purchased in the Rue Bayard, not far from the Champs Elysées, where a small church was constructed at considerable expense, the cornerstone being laid on September 12 1863. The Rev. Mr Lamson worked ceaselessly to raise more funds, and offered a number of wealthy Americans to sponsor the stained-glass windows he wanted to install. The Princesse Murat, born Caroline Georgina Frazer in South Carolina, donated a fine copy of Titian's painting of the Entombment of Christ, to be displayed in the church. In October 1864, the Bishop of Ohio came to Paris to consecrate the new American Church in the Rue Bayard.[4]

The successful construction of the American Church was a considerable achievement for the Rev. Mr Lamson, who was admired by his flock for his praiseworthy enterprise, administrative talent and philanthropic zeal. In April 1865, the Rev. Mr Lamson held a grand service in his new church, on account of the death of President Lincoln. Since the church was full to capacity, a crowd of people had to stand outside. In a brief and eloquent address, Mr Lamson alluded feelingly to the tragic fate of the President, who was snatched away from them at the very moment when the promised land of peace was opening to his view.[5]

★

George Henry Lamson graduated from his French school in the late 1860s, and went on to become a medical student, making excellent progress at the great Paris teaching hospitals. By 1866, there had been a late-coming addition to the Lamson family: the young daughter Julia Schuyler Lamson. The Rev. Mr Lamson took a larger house in the Rue Christophe to accommodate his growing family. He was highly respected by the Episcopalists in Paris, and showed praiseworthy ecumenical tendencies, often holding meetings and conferences with clergy from other Christian persuasions.

In July 1870, France declared war on Prussia. The Rev. Mr Lamson sent his wife and two younger children to England, where they moved into lodgings at Ventnor in the Isle of Wight. Himself, he remained in Paris to look after his new church, and the 18-year-old George Henry also stayed behind. A group of

3. The American Church in the Rue Bayard, Paris, during the time it served as the Scottish Church, a postcard stamped and posted in 1910.

philanthropic Americans clubbed together to form the American Ambulance, for the purpose of helping the French wounded. Dr John Swinburne, a skilful American surgeon practicing in London, became Chief Surgeon, and Dr William E. Johnston, a fashionable American doctor practicing in Paris, became Physician. The Rev. Mr Lamson became Chaplain to the American Ambulance, and

George Henry, who had studied medicine for several years in spite of his youth, became dresser to Dr Swinburne.

There was initial optimism among the French that the war would be brought to a swift and successful conclusion, but it soon became apparent that the Prussians meant business. The French generals were either overconfident or overly pessimistic, and often at loggerheads with one another; the troops were numerous but hampered by insufficient training, poor organization and indifferent morale. The Prussians were ably led by Chancellor Otto von Bismarck and Field Marshal Helmuth von Moltke, names that have passed into military history; the soldiers, wearing their field-grey uniforms and formidable spiked helmets, were known for their discipline and bravery. Austro-Hungary did not dare to enter the war on the French side, whereas the southern German states willingly joined forces with the Prussians. The French suffered crushing early defeats at Spicheren and Wœrth. The ailing Napoleon III, who suffered badly from kidney stones, had joined the army of Marshal MacMahon, but they had to capitulate at Sedan and the Emperor became a prisoner of war. The foolhardy Marshal Bazaine, whose army had taken refuge in the fortress of Metz, also had to surrender. The Second Empire was no more, Empress Eugenie had to escape to England with the Prince Imperial, and Paris was in immediate danger from the relentless Prussian advance. Already in late September 1870, the French capital was entirely encircled by the Prussian armies.

Most members of the Diplomatic Corps left Paris as soon as they could, as did clergymen of all religious persuasions. When the *Times* wrote that at the commencement of the siege, the Protestant ministers of all denominations had left Paris, the Bishop of Ohio wrote back to announce that at least one of them had not: the Rev. Mr Lamson, rector of the American Episcopal Church, found it his duty to remain in the stricken French capital; he held services in his church that could be attended by all English-speaking Christians.[6] In December 1870, the Prussians began bombarding

4. *Napoleon III, the Empress Eugenie and Marshal MacMahon, from old cabinet cards in the author's collection.*

Paris. A shell traversed two stories in the house of the Rev. Mr Lamson in the Rue Christophe, but it did not burst, and the lives of the Rev. Gentleman and his son George Henry were saved as a consequence. In a letter, the Rev. Mr Lamson described how the bomb had entered his bedroom through the window, crushing his bed into splinters and shattering the bedside furniture, before passing through the floor and bouncing down the stairs without exploding. Had his head been on the pillow, it would have been knocked straight off, but the Hand of God had saved the Rev. Gentleman.[7]

On January 23 1871, the eloquent William Orne Lamson wrote to his friend Dr Francis Vinton, of the Trinity Church in New York: "It will be a matter of some curiosity to you at least to receive a sign of life from this environed city. I am tempted to ask at once, How goes the world without? What kingdoms and empires have fallen and risen during the last four months? Prussia has grown, so the pigeons say, from a German State into an Empire, by rolling herself like a snow-ball over this stricken country, out of which she has been freezing, starving, crushing the life … I have never worked harder than during this voluntary imprisonment. As head of the ambulance, I have been at every battle-field around Paris. My poor have tried my resources and energy to the utmost. The sick have been visited, the dying consoled, the dead buried, the penitent baptized … George is with me, and has been working as surgeon-assistant in the ambulance."[8]

★

Competently led by Dr Swinburne, who had experience from the American Civil War, the American Ambulance developed a reputation for its excellent clinical standards. It was usually the first ambulance to arrive at any battlefield near Paris, and it was said that many French officers carried cards saying that if they were wounded, they should be left into the care of the Americans. The two hundred wounded officers and men attended by the American Ambulance were kept in large tents rather than in a proper hospital, since Dr Swinburne valued the circulation of air; as a result, four out of five of his amputation cases survived. As Chaplain, the Rev. Mr Lamson travelled with the Ambulance, visiting the battlefields and helping to attend the wounded. His son George Henry assisted Dr Swinburne with youthful energy; the lack of doctors meant that he was promoted to Senior Assistant Surgeon, after showing admirable bravery when collecting wounded soldiers at the battlefield of Villejuif. One of his duties was to distribute morphine cigarettes among the wounded soldiers awaiting surgery, although one of the orderlies noted that he sometimes liked to smoke them himself. Since the French Republic valued the work of the American Ambulance very highly, the Rev. Mr Lamson received the honour of becoming a Chevalier of the Legion d'Honneur, whereas George Henry had to be content with the Bronze and Iron Crosses for conspicuous bravery in the field and distinguished service to the wounded.[9]

The Parisians withstood the lengthy Prussian siege with admirable bravery, in spite of the relentless bombardment and the severe famine resulting from the encirclement of the French capital. Cats, dogs and rats were eaten by the starving Parisians, and there is nothing to suggest that the Rev. Mr Lamson and George Henry received any preferential treatment with regard to their dietary arrangements. The staff of the American Ambulance received their rations in horseflesh. The house in the Rue Christophe was full of billeted French soldiers, for whom Mr Lamson had to supply everything but their rations of food. But Paris could not be saved: on January 28 1871, an armistice was arranged, and supplies of food were organized for the starving city. The Prussians took every opportunity to humiliate their old enemies: a victory parade was arranged along the Champs Elysées, a large war indemnity was demanded, and King Wilhelm of Prussia was crowned German Emperor in the Hall of Mirrors at the Versailles Palace.

There was deep frustration among the Parisians after their humiliation under the German jackboot. The large amounts of unemployed soldiery in Paris were soon up to some serious mischief; many of them had become socialists or anarchists, and in March 1871, they took the opportunity to overthrow

5. *King Wilhelm I of Prussia, Bismarck and Moltke, from old cabinet cards in the author's collection.*

the government of the Third Republic and proclaim the Paris Commune. A short and bloody reign of terror followed, one that saw the murder of two army generals and the Archbishop of Paris, the demolition of the Vendôme Column, and the burning down of the Tuileries Palace and the Hôtel de Ville, before the army of the Third Republic besieged Paris and vanquished the Communards. In a letter to Dr Vinton in New York, the eloquent Francophile William Orne Lamson, who had remained in Paris throughout the Commune, wrote that "God help the misguided wretches who are thus made the Ministers of their own destruction and the ruin of their own fair heritage! Paris is a pitiable spectacle. Bowed to the dust of humiliation before a victorious foreign foe, France is able to make no better peace than one that keeps the conqueror at her gates, the passive spectator of her deeper degradation in the fratricidal strife in which this great city is for the second time the disputed prize. The Germans are learning how to take the city they were unable to capture by force, and seeing the work of devastation they left half done, completed by the French themselves."[10]

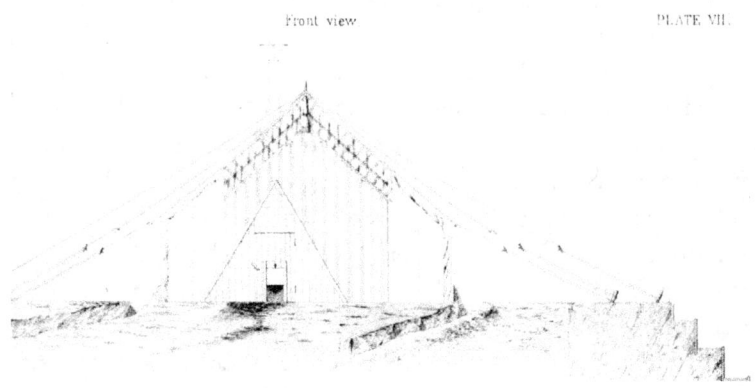

6. *A drawing of a tent from the American Ambulance.*

II.

AMERICA AND WARTIME SERVICE

At the time of the 1871 Census, the Rev. Mr Lamson and his son George Henry were recuperating at Sydney Lodge, situated at Ventnor in the Isle of Wight, with the remainder of their family, to recover from the horrors they had lived through in Paris.[1] The Rev. William Orne Lamson was now 45 years old, and his wife Julia was 40: whereas the 18-year-old war veteran George Henry was described as a medical student, his 16-year-old brother Robert Schuyler and five-year-old sister Julia were both 'scholars'. Mrs Lamson had been suffering from some obscure throat complaint, which had prevented her from speaking louder than in a whisper, but she had received treatment in London and was now on the path towards recovery.[2]

In October 1871, the Rev. Mr Lamson went to Baltimore, in order to attend the General Convention of the American Episcopal Church. He was much fêted for his wartime heroics and in New York, a testimonial dinner was held in his honour, with a speaker praising his heroism: "The services of a military and humanitarian kind, rendered by Mr Lamson during the siege, won for him, it will be remembered, at the hands of the French Government, the decoration of Knighthood of the Legion of Honour – a distinction that can scarcely fail to increase his influence for the furtherance of any work he may undertake for our church abroad."[3] After being absent until December 1871, the Rev. Mr Lamson triumphantly returned to his church in Paris, where he appeared to be much admired by his congregation for his valiant wartime record.

All was not well among the Paris Episcopalists, however, and among those who envied and resented the Rev. Mr Lamson, there were murmurations that the church finances had been haphazardly controlled in recent years. And indeed, in January 1870, a church committee had recommended that a clerk should be employed, and that the rector should be relieved of the burden of governing the financial affairs of the church. The Rev. Mr Lamson seems to have found this something of a slight, and after the turbulent war years, he did not want to engage his time in idle squabbling about church affairs. There was consternation among the Paris Episcopalists when the Rev. Mr Lamson suddenly and unexpectedly tendered his resignation on April 6 1872. The anti-Lamson fraction made sure that the resignation was accepted without the slightest protest, and the Rev. Gentleman was now a clergyman without either church or congregation.[4]

As for George Henry Lamson, he continued his medical studies in Paris after the war, spending the summer months at Ventnor with his family. In 1872, he returned to the United States, where he graduated as a Doctor of Medicine at the University of Pennsylvania, one of the leading American universities. In February 1874, he set up a small practice at Ferry Town, New York, where he was also honorary church organist, but from unspecified injurious effects to his health, brought on by his wartime service in France, he had to give this practice up. He moved to Lancaster in Pennsylvania, where he supplemented his income by 'cramming' medical students for their exams. The musical Doctor was organist and choirmaster at Christ Church, Lancaster, and a member of the Lancaster Medical Society.[5]

★

Doctor Poison

THE DOGS OF WAR.

Bull A 1. "TAKE CARE, MY MAN! IT MIGHT BE AWK'ARD IF YOU WAS TO LET 'EM LOOSE!"

1. *A caricature from* Punch, *June 17 1876, showing Russia preparing let loose the dogs of war in the Balkan states, to attack the portly, unprepared Turkey, in spite of the warning of John Bull.*

After leaving Paris, the Rev. Mr Lamson appears to have led an idle life for quite a few years, without any paid employment. He was fond of travelling, and took an interest in philanthropy and religious affairs. In August 1872, a newspaper notice tells us that he and his wife and family were on a visit to No. 3 Madeira Vale, Ventnor.[6] In October 1872, he was in Leeds, speaking at a meeting of the Association for Promoting the Union of Christendom.[7] In April 1873, he attended a ceremony at Westminster Abbey, on account of the death of the Bishop of Ohio, who had expired while on a visit to Italy.[8] The Rev. Gentleman had travelled to Florence and accompanied the body of his old friend to London, and he also arranged to supervise the transportation of the body back to the United States; the name of the ship he embarked in London was not given in the newspaper, since the superstition attached to travelling with dead bodies on board would have done harm to the sale of tickets on the transatlantic liner.[9] The Rev. Mr Lamson made it all the way to New York, where he made himself useful by marrying a young Scottish couple at a Brooklyn church on June 17.[10] He returned to Ventnor in October. In April the following year, the 'Fashionable Intelligence' column of the local newspaper could report that The Rev. W.O., Mrs and Miss Lamson had arrived at Aretum Villa, Ventnor, following a visit to Paris.[11]

The League in the Aid of the Christians of Turkey was an organization founded in December 1875 by James Lewis Farley, an Irish banker resident in London, who held strong anti-Turkish opinions, and who had sympathy for the Christians in the Balkan States, which were under Turkish rule at the time.[12] As Farley expressed it, the main objective of the League was to achieve, by every legitimate means, "the complete emancipation of the Christians of Turkey from Mussulman misrule and oppression." In 1875, there had been a revolt in Herzegovina, a province of the Ottoman Empire, which soon spread to the provinces of Bosnia and Bulgaria. The Turks were able to suppress the uprising, but in April 1876, the provinces of Serbia and Montenegro proclaimed their independence and declared war on the Ottoman Empire.[13]

James Lewis Farley worked ceaselessly in favour of the Serbs and Montenegrans, two mainly Christian countries that were rising up against the Moslem Turks. Meetings were held in Manchester, Birmingham, London and Croydon, with eloquent anti-Turkish speeches and shows of sympathy for the oppressed Christians of the Balkan states. In July 1876, Farley led a deputation from the League in the Aid of the Christians of Turkey, which was presented to Lord Derby at the Foreign Office. The Rev. William Orne Lamson also took an interest in the League and its work, and he suggested to J. Lewis Farley that they should perhaps send an ambulance, with medical supplies, to Serbia, to help the Serbian war wounded. Such an ambulance would be sorely needed, since the Turks had mobilized an army 40 000 strong, led by Abdul Kerim Pascha; due to their numerical inferiority and limited grasp of military tactics, the Serbs had already suffered some crushing defeats.

In September 1876, the League in the Aid of the Christians of Turkey made appeals for medical supplies of every description to be delivered to their office in Cockspur Street. The Rev. Mr Lamson, who was intended to go to Belgrade as the Emissary of the League, wrote to his adventurous son, inviting him to accompany him to Belgrade to supervise the medical work done under the auspices of the League, and George Henry accepted this invitation with alacrity, selling up his American property and booking his passage across the Atlantic on a fast liner. Both Lamsons were in London in late October 1876, when the Rev. Gentleman served as Chairman at two meetings of the League, delivering some rousing speeches about the practical work that was to be done in wartime Serbia.[14] On October 27 1876, George Henry left London with a consignment of medical supplies, and on November 2, the Rev. Mr Lamson followed him, with letters from Mr Farley to M. Ristitch, the Serbian Foreign Minister, and to Archbishop Michael of Belgrade.

2. *A map of the theatre of war in the Balkans, from the Daily News, July 7 1876.*

*

On November 11, J. Lewis Farley could announce that "the Rev. Mr Lamson, who left London on the 2nd instant with money and stores sent out by the League, has now arrived in Belgrade. Mr Lamson is well known for his labours amongst the sick and wounded during the siege of Paris, and will, as our representative, personally distribute amongst the suffering Christians in Servia whatever funds the Council may be enabled to send him."[15] The Rev. Mr Lamson met the Foreign Minister and Archbishop Michael, to deliver the letters entrusted to him. George Henry first served in the Moravian Valley, where he saw much action on the battlefield, and had a rib broken by a stray shell. He was then formally commissioned by the Serbian government as a military surgeon, and posted to the hospital at the city of Semendria, on the right bank of the Danube.

The Rev. Mr Lamson could report back to the League that "My son, Dr Lamson, had been, meanwhile, commissioned by the Government, and assigned to duty at the hospital at Semendria. While waiting for the goods I had ordered to be made, I went with him to Semendria to look into the condition of the wounded. The Servian hospitals everywhere betray the most elementary knowledge of medical science and of proper hygienic conditions, and this at Semendria we found to be no exception to the rule."[16] If the Rev. Mr Lamson and George Henry had got access to the American newspapers in Belgrade, they would have been in for some serious bad news in the 'Deaths' column of the *New York Times*: "LAMSON – Oct. 18, in Darfour, Upper Egypt, of malarious fever, aged 21 years, Major Robert Schuyler Lamson, C.E., of the Egyptian Army, son of Rev. W.O. Lamson, of Paris, and grandson of the late Robert Schuyler, of New York." Clearly, Dr Lamson's younger brother had graduated as an engineer in the United States, and then gone to make his fortune in the Egyptian Army, advancing rapidly through its ranks before having his life and career ended by a tropical disease.[17]

As brave and energetic in a wartime crisis as he was lazy and slipshod in civilian life, George Henry Lamson took charge of the military hospital at Semendria and improved its hygienic conditions as well as he could, remembering what he had learnt from Dr Swinburne in the Franco-Prussian War. He was a skilful military surgeon, and an expert in stemming the flow of blood from serious wounds, and in performing amputations. There was no lack of wounded soldiers to treat, since the Serbian fight for independence was going from bad to worse: the Turks were attacking in force, and in October and early November, they were threatening to overwhelm the Serbian forces altogether. There was much anti-Turkish feeling in Russia at this time, and the Russian government of course kept a close eye at the Balkan rebellion. After the Russian army had mobilized, the government threatened to declare war on the Ottoman Empire if there were not an immediate truce, followed by negotiations for peace. These negotiations lasted until January 15 1877, when there was peace between Serbia and the Ottoman Empire.

As peace was being negotiated, the Rev. Mr Lamson was making plans to return to London. Both he and J. Lewis Farley had been awarded the Gold Cross of the Order of the Takovo, in recognition of their services to the cause of the Christians of Turkey. In a report to the League in the Aid of the Christians of Turkey, the Rev. Gentleman wrote that "My son, Dr Lamson, remains in Servia, holding the honourable position of chief of

3. *A view of Semendria, from the*
Illustrated London News, *August 5 1876.*

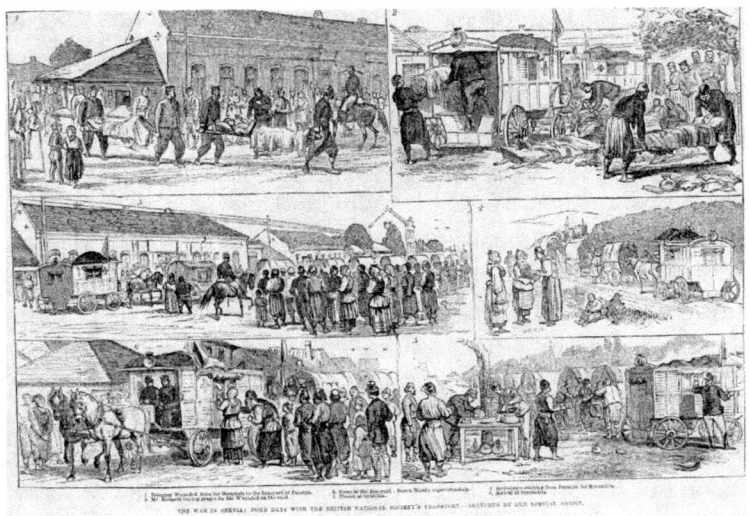

4. Ambulances on their way to Semendria, from the Illustrated London News, *December 9 1876.*

the hospital at Semendria. He is the envoy of the League, and remains as a continued proof of the zeal of your organization for the cause it was founded to serve."[18] Dr Lamson remained with the wounded in Semendria until late February 1877, when he was awarded a Gold Cross and Medal for his bravery and medical skill, to be followed by a hero's welcome at a function for the League in Aid of the Christians of Turkey in London.

*

Quite exhausted and unwell after his lengthy wartime service abroad, George Henry Lamson decided to travel back to the United States, for his health to recover. He spent much time with the Rev. Irving M'Elroy, the Rector of Christ Church, Rouse's Point in the State of New York, an old friend of his father's. The Rev. M'Elroy was astounded when one evening, the Doctor asked him to administer to him a dose of morphine hypodermically, saying that he had learnt to like it in Serbia. Having spent several months in the United States, the Doctor returned to England, and spent the remaining summer months with his parents and sister at Ventnor. But as Dr Lamson was recuperating, all was not well back in the Balkan States. The Russians were of the opinion that Turkey was the Sick Man of Europe, and their approach to that particular invalid was that he should promptly have his Balkan possessions permanently amputated. Pan-Slavist Russians, who urged war against Turkey to back the Balkan Slavs, and to recoup territorial losses from the Crimean War, soon got into a position of influence. After an agreement had been made that Austro-Hungary would not interfere in the Balkan crisis, Russia declared war against the Ottoman Empire on April 24 1877.

Russian troops swiftly entered Romania, where they were welcomed as liberators: the Romanians declared their independence from Turkey and joined the war on the Russian side. The Bulgarians and Serbs also rose up to join the fight for independence against the Turks. The Ottoman Empire still had a formidable army, however, and their recent triumphs in Serbia provided them with some much-needed confidence. After some fierce fighting, the Russians established themselves on enemy territory, but it looked like if it was going to be a lengthy war, as the Turks entrenched themselves in a line of powerful fortresses.

J. Lewis Farley, and the League in the Aid of the Christians of Turkey, received the news of the Russo-Turkish War with enthusiasm. In August 1877, the philanthropic Rev. Mr Lamson became one of the Hon. Treasurers for the Sick and Wounded Russian Soldiers' Relief Fund, operating from the League's headquarters at No. 14 Cockspur Street.[19] Money, blankets and medical supplies were collected all over the country, since although the Russians themselves were viewed with scepticism by most Britons, there was a good deal of sympathy for the oppressed Balkan Christians. In early October, J. Lewis Farley could report that both the Rev. Mr Lamson and his son George Henry had left London: the former destined for St Petersburg and the latter for Bucharest.[20] On October 12, the Rev. Mr Lamson was received in a special audience by the Empress of Russia, at Tsarskoe Selo.[21] The help from the Sick and Wounded Russian Soldiers' Relief Fund was to be channelled through the Russian Red Cross, and the Rev. Gentleman visited their headquarters in St Petersburg to make sure the material intended for the frontline was well taken care of. In early November, he wrote home to J. Lewis Farley to report that the Empress had once more honoured him with a private audience, during which she had spoken highly of the philanthropic zeal of the Sick and Wounded Russian Soldiers' Relief Fund.[22] On November 17, the Rev. Mr Lamson left St Petersburg to join his son in Bucharest.

George Henry Lamson arrived in Bucharest on October 12, as the head of an English military hospital, and emissary of the Sick and Wounded Russian Soldiers' Relief Fund. Together with his colleague Dr Mower, he took charge of the hospital and oversaw its activities. Since fighting was still fierce, as the Russians were besieging the Turkish fortresses in the Balkans, the influx of wounded Russian and Romanian soldiers was very considerable. On November 5, it was reported that the English Relief Fund Hospital had received its full complement of 30 wounded Romanians, selected by Dr Lamson in person among the worst cases he could find at the Russian Military Hospital.[23] A report to the League in the Aid of the Christians of Turkey said that "Doctor Lamson has had wide experience in his vocation, for he served through the Franco-German war, and last year through the Servian war. He represents Mr. Lewis Farley's Committee, and enjoys the unique advantage of being the only foreign surgeon recognized by the Russian Red Cross Society. In the latter capacity he devotes a portion of his time to the Russian Central Military Hospital in Bucharest."[24]

THE WAR IN THE EAST—BARON MUNDY'S CHAIR CONVEYANCE FOR THE WOUNDED, SEMENDRIA

5. *A wounded soldier is carried to Semendria, from the* Graphic, *September 30 1876.*

In late November, a Bucharest correspondent of the *Daily News* went to see the English Relief Fund Hospital: "Up a staircase, through a room set apart for stores, and we are shown into the wards. After the dirt and turmoil of a Bucharest street, the quiet order and cleanliness is very marked. The object of the hospital is to succour the Romanian wounded, and it was started about two months ago by Dr and Mrs Mower. The staff consists of Dr Mower and Dr Lamson; the number of beds about 30." There was a proper bathroom, a contraption some of the wounded soldiers had never before seen, and also a kitchen and offices, the doctor's room and an operating room. Most cases were bullet wounds, and since gangrene was a danger, the two doctors were adept in carrying out amputations. The correspondent greatly admired the work of Dr Lamson and Dr Mower, and thought their hospital in Bucharest a model enterprise.[25]

An English surgeon who met Dr Lamson in Bucharest later had nothing but good to say about him: "I was myself a witness of the good work he did in Roumania during the autumn of 1877, when he placed his time and talents unreservedly at the disposal of Queen, then Princess, Elizabeth. It was at this time that I made his personal acquaintance, for, although I had frequently heard of him as an able and gallant volunteer surgeon in Servia during the previous year's campaign, we had never chanced to meet until my lamented friend, Mr M'Gahan, introduced Mr Lamson to me in Bucharest, to the best of my remembrance a few days before the Roumanian army crossed the Danube. At our very first meeting Lamson impressed me favourably. His appearance and manners were alike eminently prepossessing. Further acquaintance with him, which soon assumed a character of intimacy, confirmed by first impressions. I found him a well-bred and highly-educated man, 'full of excellent differences,' extremely sweet-tempered and cheerful, and a decided acquisition to the foreign colony attracted to Bucharest by the stirring events of that sensational epoch, as well as to Roumanian society, in which he was received with open arms, as some small acknowledgement of his assiduous

6. *Turkish troops are transported by railway in the Russo-Turkish War, from the* Graphic, *September 29 1877.*

and disinterested service in the hospitals and ambulances, hastily improvised in and near Bucharest as soon as the dread tidings of the Grivitza assault reached that capital."

Dr Lamson's generous friend continued: "An excellent French scholar, and possessing more than an elementary knowledge of one or two other Continental languages, Lamson was able to hold his own in the salons of some of the fair leaders of Bucharest society, as well as to confer freely with his professional *confrères*, natives to the soil. I may with truth say of him that he won golden opinions from all manner of men. Davila, the Inspector-general of hospitals, and Marcovich, the fashionable doctor of the Roumanian *grande monde*, alike held him in high esteem, and courted his society. He was a frequent guest at the British Agency, and Her Highness the Princess honoured him with her particular notice. At one time and another I saw a great deal of him, and came – as I thought then and still think – to know him well. During a brief illness, due to over fatigue and the depressing effect of a

7. *A Russian cavalry charge, from the* Graphic, *September 29 1877.*

fierce Roumanian summer, I was his debtor for many judicious and tender kindnesses. Nothing seemed to give him so much pleasure as to be of any use to his friends and acquaintances. His fund of anecdote was inexhaustible; but, although a spirited and willing *raconteur*, he invariably observed a modest reserve with regard to his own achievements in past campaigns – achievements which, as I learned from other sources, had upon many occasions redounded to his honour."[26]

Later, the adventurous Dr Lamson was at Plevna on transport service, and returned conveying Turkish prisoners, suffering terrible privations after being snowed up for six days without any food. The Prince and Princess of Romania both personally thanked him for his valiant service in favour of the wounded soldiers, awarding him the Order of the Star of Romania (4th class) and the Order of Medjidie (5th class). Under pressure from Britain, Russia accepted the truce offered by the Ottoman Empire on January 31 1878, but their troops continued to move towards Constantinople. When a fleet of Royal Navy battleships made an appearance, the Russians stopped at San Stefano, and a settlement of peace was made, in which Romania, Serbia and Montenegro gained their independence, and Bulgaria its autonomy. Dr Lamson remained with his wounded soldiers until March 1878, when he returned to London.

III.

ROTHERFIELD AND BOURNEMOUTH

After his return from Bucharest, George Henry Lamson went to Edinburgh, where he spent two months brushing up his medical education and attending various lectures, before sitting his final examinations. In what appears to have been his first attempt, he graduated Licentiate of the Royal College of Physicians and Licentiate of the Royal College of Surgeons of Edinburgh at the April and May sittings.[1] Cheered by this success, which gave him the license to practice in Britain, he lost no time before purchasing a medical practice in the village of Rotherfield, Sussex.

Rotherfield was (and still is) a small village, situated not far from Crowborough, and George Henry Lamson was its only doctor. He took a large and ancient house known as Horse Grove, situated off South Street, which had formerly been the home of an old practitioner named Dr McIntyre.[2] Initially, Dr Lamson got on well with the locals, impressing them with his apparent wealth, grand house and distinguished wartime record. He was employed as medical officer for the Rotherfield and Mayfield Orphanages. A full staff of servants was employed at Horse Grove, and the grandiose Doctor spent vigorously to furnish the house. During his summer holiday in Ventnor, Dr Lamson, who was himself still just 26 years old, met the 25-year-old Miss Kate George John, who belonged to a wealthy Welsh family hailing

1. Dr George Henry Lamson, from a drawing by the obscure American artist P.B. Whelpley, reproduced by H.L. Adam, The Trial of George Henry Lamson.

from Swansea. In October, the *British Medical Journal* had the following announcement to make: "LAMSON – JOHN. – On the 14th inst., at Holy Trinity Church, Ventnor, by the Rev. W.O. Lamson, M.A., late of Paris (father of the bride-groom), assisted by the Rev. A.L.B. Peile, M.A., Vicar of Holy Trinity, and by the Rev. H.T. Maddock, M.A., Rector of Bonchurch, George Henry Lamson, Esq., M.D., L.R.C.P.Ed, L.R.S.C.Ed., of Rotherfield, Sussex, to Kate George, eldest daughter of the late William John, Esq., of Swansea."[3]

The John family is worthy of a short discourse. The 1861 Census has the 45-year-old Mr William John living in a large terraced house at No. 7 Brunswick Place, Swansea, with his family. He is recorded to have been born in Pembroke, just like his nine years younger wife Eliza. Kate George John was their eldest child, and she had the younger sister Margaret Eliza and the younger brothers Sidney Twyning and Hubert William. The youngest brother Percy Malcolm John was born in December 1862, and baptized at St Mary's Parish Church, Swansea, on January 19 1863. After William John had died in July 1865, his widow Eliza followed him into the grave on April 26 1869, from pulmonary tuberculosis, at her house in No. 10 Cornwallis Crescent, Clifton, leaving the five children orphans and wards in Chancery; Frederick King Laverton, of Bristol, and

2. *The Holy Trinity Church, Ventnor, where George Henry Lamson got married.*

3. Saint Mary's Church, Swansea, where Percy Malcolm John was christened in January 1863.

David Ormond, of No. 23 Cannon Street in London, were the executors.[4] The 1871 Census lists Kate George John and her younger sister Margaret Eliza as scholars at Skidmore's School, in Rickmanworth, Hertfordshire. There were six other pupils, and the school was at 'The Pines', a large house in the High Street. Sidney Twyning John died at Elizabeth Cottage, Ventnor, on April 22 1873, from pulmonary tuberculosis according to his death certificate. Margaret Eliza John married the civil service clerk William Greenhill Chapman in 1877; she would have at least one son and live on for several decades. The health of the two remaining brothers left much to be desired, however: whereas Hubert William John also suffered from tuberculosis, the youngest brother Percy Malcolm had a severe scoliosis, a curvature of the spine serious enough to render him paralyzed in both legs.

In 1878, Percy Malcolm John was installed as a pupil at Blenheim House School, a large establishment situated at No. 1-2 St George's Road, Wimbledon. This boarding school had been inaugurated in 1872, and consisted of two large town houses linked by a corridor; it was run by the principal Mr William Henry Bedbrook, a former senior master at South Hackney College, and there were several junior masters on the premises. Percy slept on the second floor, and since the schoolroom was on the lower ground floor, he was equipped with a wheelchair on each floor to be capable of locomotion. The other boys took turns to carry him up and down stairs in the morning and in the evening. Percy shared a dormitory with three other boys. At the age of 16, he was older than most of the other pupils, although his education may well have been somewhat backward when he joined the school. He took part in the lessons as well as he could, and even tried to play sports with the other pupils, wheeling himself about seated in his wheelchair. Apart from his scoliosis, Percy was in good physical health, albeit often despondent about his prospects in life. His guardian, the civil service clerk William Greenhill Chapman, must have thought Blenheim House School a cheap and convenient place for Percy to stay, and the unfortunate lad could look forward to several more years on the premises. The John family was a wealthy one, and the will of Eliza John dictated that as long as the sons Hubert and Percy were minors, their inheritances should be held in trust while they were under age. The jovial George Henry Lamson seems to have got on quite well with his three brothers-in-law, all of whom he invited for regular visits to his large house in Rotherfield, or to the house the Lamson family took in Ventnor during the summer months.

Dr Lamson lived contentedly in Rotherfield with his wife for the remainder of 1878, and well into 1879. On June 24 1879, there was a jolly family gathering at Horse Grove, with Kate Lamson's brother Hubert William John and sister Margaret Chapman coming to visit. Although Hubert suffered from tuberculosis, he was obviously capable of locomotion and fit enough to travel. There was tragedy when the 18-year-old Hubert died suddenly and unexpectedly during this visit. George Henry Lamson wrote his death certificate, giving the cause of death as pulmonary consumption and amyloid degeneration. Mrs M.E. Chapman, sister of the deceased, of No. 29 Nicoll Road, Harlesden, London, present at the death, came in handy as a witness. As a result of Hubert's demise while still a minor, Kate Lamson inherited £479 in India Stocks and £269 in Consols, money that went into the Doctor's pockets since there was no Married Women's Property Act back in 1879. Delighted to have got his hands on some hard cash, he soon spent much of it on his various amusements.[5]

On August 20 1879, the *Standard* newspaper could announce that "LAMSON – August 14, Horsegrove House, Rotherfield, Tunbridge-wells, the wife of Geo. H. Lamson, Esq., M.D., late of New York, of a daughter."[6] This daughter was christened Agnes Margaret Schuyler Lamson. But by this time, all was not well at Horse Grove. Albeit an excellent military surgeon, George Henry Lamson found rural general practice pointless and dull. He was fond of travel and holidays, and had a firm dislike for hard graft and honest toil. Since his bedside manner was far from the best, the locals found him flippant, inattentive and unreliable. He often showed his contempt for the trivial complaints he was presented with. There were several instances of doctors being called from Tunbridge Wells since Lamson could not be relied upon to attend. Soon, there were unpleasant rumours circulating about the carelessness and inattention of this Transatlantic quack

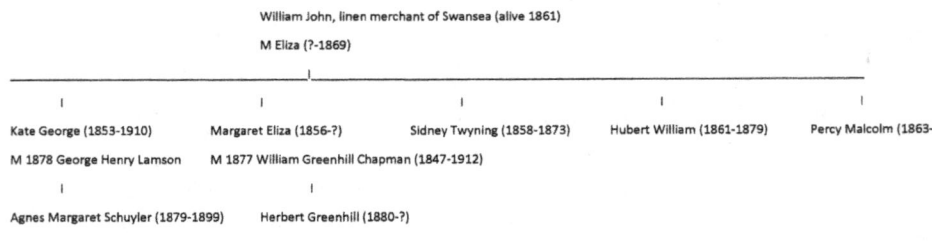

4. *The John pedigree.*

5. High Street, Rotherfield, a postcard stamped and posted in 1905.

doctor, and although Lamson was never prosecuted or officially complained against, his position in Rotherfield soon became wholly untenable.[7] Furthermore, feathers had been ruffled in the Sussex medical circles after Lamson had placed upon his nameplate the name of a surgeon living at Crowborough, without that gentleman's knowledge or consent. Dr Lamson decided to leave Horse Grove and Rotherfield, for good, and to make use of the remainder of his wife's inheritance money to purchase a practice in a bigger town, where he hoped the patients would be less grumpy and demanding. When a London doctor came to inquire about the Rotherfield practice, the canny Lamson had employed some local children to keep ringing the bell, to give the impression that he had quite a healthy supply of patients. After this stratagem had the desired effect, the practice sold in late September 1879.[8]

In 1879, the globetrotting Rev. Mr Lamson was staying in Florence with his wife and daughter. He noticed that the Rev. Pierce Connelly, the Rector of St James' American Church, was getting increasingly infirm, and offered to help him managing the church. From 1880 onwards, the Rev. Mr Lamson was in charge of the church, living in Florence with his family, and renting rooms adjacent to the chapel. Thus the Doctor would be without his father and mentor during a troubled period of his life.[9]

6. *St James American Church, Florence, where the Rev. Mr Lamson worked from 1879 until 1883.*

*

George Henry Lamson wanted to go to Ventnor, where his family was well known, but since this town already had a full complement of doctors, there was no practice to be had. Instead, in October 1879, he made use of the remaining £400 of Mrs Lamson's inheritance money to buy an established general practice in Bournemouth, with consulting rooms at the terraced town house at No. 1 Beaumont Terrace, Poole Hill. With his usual grandiosity, the Doctor took a fine detached residence known as 'Hursley', situated at the corner of Poole Road and Cambridge Road, next to St Michael's Church.[10] Mrs Lamson and young Agnes were installed there, with a full staff of servants to look after their needs.

A handsome, personable man, with regular features, dark hair and a short beard, George Henry Lamson initially made good progress in the Hampshire medical circles. He joined the Bournemouth Medical Society, got a commission as a Lieutenant in the 1st Bournemouth Hants Artillery Volunteers, hob-nobbed in society and joined several social clubs. In October 1879, he met Mr William Stevenson, the editor of the *Bournemouth Observer*, and these two became good friends. The Doctor also befriended the surveyor Arthur Joseph Salter, the valuer William Arthur Marshall and the gentleman Radclyffe Radclyffe-Hall.[11] His supply of patients to treat, for all kinds of maladies, was a steady one, since many of them had come with the practice. The problem was that just like he had done at Rotherfield, Dr Lamson got bored with the often trivial complaints he was facing. He was fond of travel and holidays, and no friend of hard work. He valued his night's sleep, and much resented it when he had to make calls in the middle of the night after one of his patients had been taken ill. In early October 1880, he made an effort to improve his position by applying to become Medical Officer of Health in Bournemouth, but Mr H.P. Nunn, the sitting incumbent, was preferred to him.[12]

A little knowledge is a dangerous thing, and the same rule applies to medical knowledge. In his busy wartime service, Dr Lamson had been brave, effective and skilful, but in civilian Bournemouth idleness, he had much time to take notice of his own symptoms of disease, and to make a provisional and worrying diagnosis. The hypochondriacal Doctor noticed that his memory was failing, that his levels of concentration were low, that he constantly felt dizzy, and that he suffered from numbness and pins and needles in all four extremities. The worst thing was that the state of his bowels, with severe constipation in spite of his relative youth. Dr Lamson was fond of consulting his professional brethren about his various complaints, albeit annoyed when they found nothing much wrong with him.

There was fierce competition between the Bournemouth doctors, quite a few of whom did not appreciate the flashy and grandiose Dr Lamson, whose entry in the Medical Directory pointed out his many foreign decorations. It also boasted that he was a Doctor of Medicine of Paris and Licentiate of the Royal College of Physicians of London, and that he possessed a certificate in Sanitary Sciences from Cambridge University. Dr William Frazer, Hon. Secretary of the Bournemouth Medical Society, who had no liking for Dr Lamson, made it his business to check whether Lamson's medical credentials were correct. He found that although the Doctor's 1878 Edinburgh titles were fully valid, he had no claim to any Paris doctorate, or any degree from the Royal College of Physicians of London; the Cambridge sanitary certificate was bogus as well. For a doctor to make use of medical degrees to which he was not entitled was a heinous offence in those days, and the gloating Dr Frazer wrote a disagreeable letter to Dr Lamson, saying that his name would be perpetually expurged from the roll of Members of the Bournemouth Medical Society.[13] The General Medical Council and the General Council of Medical Education & Registration were corresponded with, but they decided to refer the case to the Royal Colleges of Physicians and Surgeons of Edinburgh, who in turn responded that since Lamson's Edinburgh degrees were genuine, they did not feel justified in taking any action against him for fraudulently making use of titles granted by other bodies. The *Lancet* commented on the case as late as February 1882, at a time when Dr Lamson stood before a higher tribunal, accused of causing much greater mischief than lying about his medical qualifications.[14]

In 1880 and 1881, some of his patients found Dr Lamson's behaviour more than a little odd. Mr Arthur John Hawkes consulted Dr Lamson on December 8 1880, for his wife who had just given birth. When the Doctor came, he looked much distracted, and did not inquire as to the well-being of the mother and child. He kept pacing up and down the sick-bed, holding his head, before abruptly sitting down on the pillow just by the wife's head, exclaiming "Mr Hawkes, will you excuse me, I am feeling very strangely in my head this morning!" Miss Lydia Humphreys, a spinster who went to Bournemouth with her invalid sister,

7. *A postcard stamped and posted in 1910, showing Poole Hill and St Michael's Church. Dr Lamson's practice at No. 1 Beaumont Terrace is the first house with a shop extension to the ground floor, although it is likely to have had its original front garden back in the 1870s. Beyond the church, the tall trees of Dr Lamson's grand detached house 'Hursley' can be seen; some of these trees remain today, although the house itself has been demolished.*

8. *St Michael's Church, Bournemouth, from an old postcard; the roof of Dr Lamson's house 'Hursley' can clearly be seen to the left of the church.*

consulted Dr Lamson on January 6 1881, since she was worried about her sister's chest. When the Doctor came calling at their lodgings, he seemed strangely preoccupied, and sat tapping his fingers. He kept up a light conversation, asking the two sisters whether they were comfortable in their apartments, but made no effort to examine the invalid's chest. On a later occasion, when the concerned Miss Humphreys told the Doctor that her sister had been coughing blood, he merely laughed in her face.[15]

In February 1881, Dr Lamson's behaviour went from bad to worse. He wrote to his friend Radclyffe Radclyffe-Hall, the son of a Torquay doctor and a gentleman resident at 'Sunny Lawn', Durley Road, Bournemouth, to inform him that his wife Marie had a somewhat interesting past. She had once belonged to the Paris *demi-monde* and had been the mistress of a millionaire named Alphonse Prévost-Paradol. In 1871 and 1872, Lamson had often seen these two taking exercise in the Bois de Boulogne, or attending the opera together. Marie had been known as 'Madame Céléstine' and had been 'kept' by Prévost-Paradol in an apartment near Rue Balzac. During the 'Carnaval' of 1872, Marie had been going out with other men, however, and this had angered Prévost-Paradol. When he found her with a young man at the Bal Masqué of the Grand Opéra, he had challenged his rival to a duel. The other man turned out to be a crack shot, however, and Prévost-Paradol was mortally wounded. Lamson claimed to have attended this duel, in the capacity of surgeon, although he had been unable to save the life of the gunned-down millionaire. Prévost-Paradol had provided well for his mistress: in spite of her unfaithfulness, he had given her a magnificent apartment, and she was the envy of the *demi-monde* with her beautiful toilettes and splendid horses and carriages. When Lamson had been introduced to her at 'Sunny Lawn' in July 1880, he had immediately recognized her as the notorious 'Madame Céléstine', particularly since she whistled an air just like the Paris courtesan, accompanying herself on the piano. Since Lamson had no reason to make such a story up, Radclyffe-Hall confronted his wife, and there was an estrangement between them, but afterwards the husband discovered that the story was a tissue of falsehoods. The novelist Charles Reade added that he had known a man named Lucien-Anatole Prévost Paradol, but he had been an author and journalist rather than a millionaire; nor had he been in the habit of fighting duels, and he committed suicide in New York in 1870, before the time period alluded to by Lamson.[16]

In addition to his fraudulent use of medical qualifications, strange behaviour towards his patients, and libellous statement about his friend's wife, Dr Lamson was a very bad business man. He opened an account in the Bournemouth branch of the Wilts and Dorset Banking Company in early November 1880, but it was closed in January 1881, after the Doctor had issued some dishonoured cheques. He kept spending extravagantly, and since his income from the practice dwindled alarmingly in late 1880, he had to borrow money from various friends and acquaintants. He soon owed the editor William Stevenson more than £100, and the chartered accountant Thomas Cullan £200. The upholsterer James Croome, who was owed in excess of £63 for goods supplied, issued a writ and put in an execution in March 1881, but he was too late. Edward Wyse Rebbeck, the agent for the owner of 'Hursley', had not been paid any rent for 1881, so he sent the bailiffs in and all Dr Lamson's effects were seized and sold at auction to the highest bidder. The sum of £35 was made use of to pay the landlord his rent, and the balance of £40 17s. was handed over to the Sheriff for use towards other executions. The upholsterer Croome received £14 6s. 7d. of this money, but he would never see the remainder of the money he was owed; neither Stevenson nor Cullan would ever receive a penny of what they had lent to the deceitful Dr Lamson.[17]

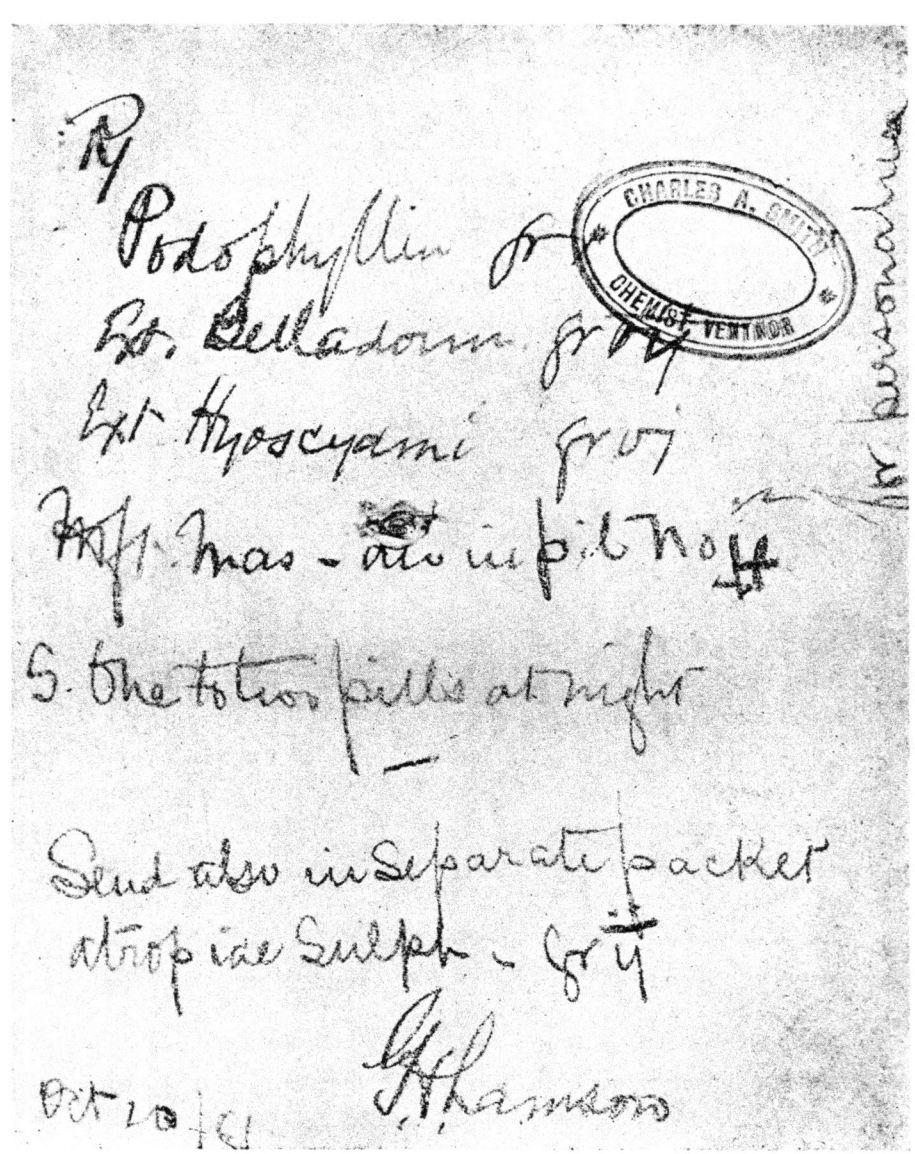

9. One of Dr Lamson's prescriptions, from W. Wood,
Survivors Tales of Famous Crimes *(London 1916).*

IV.

AMERICA, SHANKLIN AND LONDON

After his disgrace in Bournemouth, Dr Lamson made haste to depart the country for the United States, leaving his wife and daughter behind in a cheap hotel. Even though he had no income at all, and the bailiffs had come to call to take his effects away, he still possessed enough money to purchase a one-way railway ticket to Liverpool, leaving Bournemouth on April 5 and arriving in London the following day. According to his pocket diary, he took a room at Wood's Hotel, Furnival's Inn, which he initially thought "A capital house, isn't dear", but after he had tried to haggle about the bill, he was unceremoniously asked to leave: "Manner & words there very unpleasant. Shall never darken those doors again." The Doctor came to Liverpool on April 7, where he bought a ticket on the steamer *City of Berlin*, which "sailed almost immediately. Strong breeze, tho' bright and clear." On April 8, he went ashore at Queenstown in Ireland, taking a stroll along the harbour. The ship arrived in New York on April 18. On board, the Doctor presented himself to the ship's surgeon, saying that he had sold his practice in Bournemouth due to ill health.[1]

Dr Gustavus S. Winston, the medical director of the Mutual Life Insurance Company in New York, had been introduced to George Henry Lamson by his father at Ventnor in June 1880. In March 1881, he received a letter from the Rev. Mr Lamson that George Henry was on his way to New York, to consult him about his failing health. And indeed, in late April, George Henry presented himself at Dr Winston's office, so changed in both appearance and manner that the startled New York doctor failed to recognize him. The Rev. Mr Lamson had informed him that he had reason to believe that during his stay in Bournemouth, George Henry had formed the habit of using injections of excessive amounts of morphine for the relief of pain, and that this pernicious habit had grown upon him as to materially impede his mind. Dr Winston found Lamson unable to converse fluently for any length of time, with a very marked change for the worse as to the state of his brain.[2] Dr Lamson declared his intention to travel on to visit some old friends of his, however, and he did not want to stay in New York for treatment. Poor Mrs Lamson wrote him some pathetic letters, declaring herself willing to share a life of poverty, as long as he allowed her to join him in the United States, but the cruel Doctor snubbed her.

Dr Lamson once more went to see his old friend, the Rev. Irving M'Elroy, at Rouse's Point. As the Doctor came off the train, the Rev. Mr M'Elroy was much struck with his altered appearance. His face was flushed, his eyes dull and heavy, and his walk unsteady like if he had been inebriated. The ailing Doctor complained incessantly of headaches, dizziness, constipation and insomnia, and seemed a shadow of his former vigorous self. He complained of coughing blood, as a result of his chest wound in the Serbo-Turkish War, he believed. Once, he went to the local pharmacy with a prescription for a morphine mixture, for his own use; the quantity was such that the clerk asked him what use he intended to make of it. In M'Elroy's house, Dr Lamson spent most of his time lying on a sofa in the drawing-room, either sleeping or reading a book. He staggered up to bed in the wee hours. M'Elroy strongly suspected that he was making use of his hypodermic syringe to inject the morphine he had purchased, since he seemed constantly under the influence of a drug, with a flushed face and dilated pupils. Mrs Kate M'Elroy was ill at the time, and Lamson wanted to prescribe for her, but his condition was such that the Rev. Mr M'Elroy did not allow him to administer medicines to any member of the household.[3] During his stay with the M'Ilroy's, Dr Lamson wrote to his Bournemouth friend Thomas Cullan, whom he owed £200: "My dear Brother Cullan, – I am just only off a sick bed, which has very nearly ended my earthly career, and I feel I must send you a few lines just to tell you of the cause of my long silence. My obligation to you hangs constantly over my head, and by the next European mail (early next week) I trust to be able to send a more satisfactory letter. In the greatest haste, gratefully and sincerely yours, and with best fraternal greetings, Geo. H. Lamson." But Cullan would never hear from Dr Lamson again.[4]

Mrs Kate M'Elroy had known Dr Lamson since the autumn of 1871, but had not seen him since 1877. She also noticed a terrible change in his appearance: once his carriage had been very erect and soldier-like, but now his body was stooped, with the left shoulder higher than the right one. He could sleep all day and remain awake all night. Once, she saw him injecting morphine, and took the syringe away from him; when she said "You look like a man who is going mad!" a look of terror passed over his face. The Doctor had brought with him a capacious medicine-chest, which he made liberal use of to treat his own various complaints; since the bottles were mostly unlabelled, there was soon a serious mishap, when he took a large dose of laudanum in mistake for chlorodyne. He also had a large quantity of pills, which he had not marked as to their contents and provenance; when he told Mrs M'Ilroy that an unmarked box full of sugar-coated pills were either quinine or morphine, but that he did not remember which, she was so alarmed for the accident-prone Doctor's safety that she threw the entire box into the lake, for the fishes to find out their proper constituent. Dr Lamson sometimes took small amounts of brandy, but was otherwise abstemious. His conversation was sometimes clear and coherent, and his memory good, but at times, he was talking wildly and incoherently, and made little sense. The two M'Elroys were not sorry to see Dr Lamson depart their house on June 23, since he had been quite a burden to them.

After Dr Lamson's departure, the worried M'Elroy wrote to the Rev. Mr Lamson in Florence. The Rev. Gentleman wrote back on July 15: "Dear Mr M'Elroy, – I have your letter of yesterday, and again thank you for the candour and clearness with which you have written me upon this sad subject. It enables me to deal with the whole problem more effectively than I would otherwise have done. Many things are now clear to me which before were inexplicable, and my only hope is that the fearful habit has not gotten too strong a hold upon George to be broken. He has plainly been living for some time upon unrealities, and exposing himself to grave misunderstanding by his fantasies. Still, I hope by care and with the blessing of God, we can grapple successfully with the evil, and give George back to his work, for which he has such high qualifications. It must be a work of time and care. We know for the first time the nature of his trouble, for I believe this destructive, morbid appetite to have been the cause of all his ill-health and consequent break-up in life."[5]

Dr Lamson next went to stay with his uncle Oliver L. Barbour, a councellor-at-law residing at Saratoga Springs. Mr Barbour's daughter Kate thought the Doctor a very queer customer indeed. She later declared that "He told me he suffered constant pain in the head, in consequence of a scalp wound received in the Eastern war. At times his conversation was entirely rational and reasonable, and then he would suddenly, in the midst of a sentence, change on to a new topic, and relate marvellous and incredible adventures and experiences with a wandering, restless, and exceedingly painful appearance in his eyes." Florence M. Schuyler, another daughter of Barbour's, also met Dr Lamson, whom she had known since his childhood. He seemed very much changed in his manner, and told her some fantastic stories about his mother's family, like that his maternal grandmother had been a foreign princess, expressing surprise that she did not already know this. At times, he acted so strangely that she had to apologize to some friends of the family who had come visiting.[6]

While staying with the Barbours, Dr Lamson wrote a long letter to a certain Mrs Millett, who lived at Bramley Lodge, Surbiton Hill. It would appear that she was a wealthy lady whom the Doctor had befriended in happier days. He wrote that "My health has improved very much since I came here, but it never again will be wise or prudent for me to undertake working a practice like that I so recently gave up in Bournemouth with its heavy amount of night work and duties of a wearisome or tedious and irregular character, but I have every reason to hope and believe I shall before very long be able to work a little in my profession, if in a genial climate." He contrasted his current state of impaired health with the heady days of vigour in Rotherfield and Bournemouth, where they had spent so many happy hours together. He wanted to leave sunless England, for good, and take up permanent residence in Florence with his father and family, to work as doctor to the English-speaking expatriates and tourists there. Mrs Millett had an invalid son named Frank, and the Doctor promised to take good care of his health if he agreed to join him in Florence to enjoy the sunny climate.[7]

*

On July 2, Dr Lamson left New York on the steamship *City of Berlin*, arriving in Liverpool about two weeks later. He travelled on to London, where he consulted a certain Dr Millar, of Upper Norwood, complaining of various diffuse neurological symptoms. It was clear to Dr Millar that the real problem was the pernicious effects of excessive subcutaneous injections of morphine and atropine, however. Disappointed with Dr Millar's diagnosis, Dr Lamson went to join his wife and parents at 'Mount Vernon', the house they had rented in Ventnor, for a summer holiday. In Ventnor, the hypochondriacal Doctor consulted Dr John Mann Williamson, complaining of emaciation and peculiar nervous symptoms. Dr Williamson found nothing wrong with his patient, except that he had a number of small abscesses on both arms, the result of using a non-sterile needle while injecting his morphine mixture.[8]

Dr Lamson's brother-in-law William Greenhill Chapman had taken some rooms in the house 'Clarence Villa' in Shanklin not far away, with his wife Margaret and her crippled brother Percy Malcolm John, who was on a summer holiday from Blenheim House School. Dr Lamson and his wife met them at Shanklin station when they arrived on August 27, and they had a jolly family gathering. The Doctor, who had returned from the United States just a few weeks earlier, declared his intention to return there in a few days. But first, he would come back to Shanklin on August 29, to say goodbye to Percy before he went to Liverpool, he said. On August 28, Dr Lamson went to the shop of Charles Albert Smith, chemist, at No. 76 High Street, to purchase some medicine: three grains of atropine, a grain of the powerful alkaloid poison aconitine, a bottle of Eau de Cologne and a stick of Pear's shaving soap. William Greenhill Chapman was out when the Doctor came to call on August 29, but when Chapman returned home, Percy was complaining of being unwell and feeling very sick and nauseous. He went to bed early and had recovered at breakfast-time the following day.[9]

Dr Lamson left Liverpool on August 30, on the steamship *City of Brussels*, arriving in New York a few weeks later. He straight away went to see Dr Gustavus Winston, who had agreed to watch over him at his office. Lamson denied using morphine, although he had done so one or two years ago, albeit never to excess. As evidence, he pointed out that his pupils were of normal size and that his arms had no marks of injections. Every day, Lamson came to Dr Winston's office, looking most gloomy and dejected. Although he knew both the clerks and Dr Winston's associate Dr Gillett, he spoke to nobody. He used to lie on the sofa for hours on end, changing his position constantly, with marked restlessness and nervousness. He tried to sleep, but could not. If Dr Winston spoke to him, he exhibited great weariness, and was barely able to reply. Dr Winston could see that Lamson's pupils were of normal size, and that they reacted properly to light, although he appreciated that with his knowledge of chemistry, the Doctor would have been able to combine morphine with atropine in order to avoid unwanted side-effects with regard to his pupils.[10] On October 6, after nearly a month of treatment, Dr Lamson could stand it no longer: he left New York on the steamship *City of Montreal*.

*

Dr Lamson arrived at Liverpool on October 17. He went to Ventnor to see his mother, and then to Bournemouth where he called on his friend, the credulous editor William Stevenson, to whom he owed £100. The suave Doctor assured Stevenson that his money would be repaid, with interest, in due course, and he left with a case of surgical instruments he had deposited with Stevenson, a travel rug, and yet another loan of £5. He decided to stay in London for a while, taking a room at Nelson's Hotel at No. 97-99 Great Portland Street. In early November, the Rev. Mr Lamson came from Florence to visit him for a few days. To get a roof over her head, Mrs Lamson was staying at a hotel near Chichester with young Agnes; her selfish husband seems to have cared little about her, concentrating on his own miseries in life.

As he sat brooding over his failures in Rotherfield and Bournemouth, and his futile travels to America, alone in his tiny room at Nelson's Hotel in the London November gloom, Dr Lamson was becoming increasingly desperate. Not long ago, he had possessed a comfortable house, a good medical practice, and a steady income; now, he had neither of these things, and was poor as a church mouse. Dr Lamson entirely lacked employment and occupation, something that did not agree with him, and we all know who it is who finds work for idle hands to do. Had the Doctor been classically inclined, he would have been reminded of the legend of the once-famous Byzantine general Belisarius, said to have been reduced to a blind beggar in his old age, having to ask passers-by 'Date obolum Belisario' – 'Give a coin to Belisarius'. Lamson had once had power over life and death, the wounded Serbian and Romanian soldiers relying upon him for their recovery like if he had been something of a deity; now, he was just yet another penniless, unemployed vagabond, struggling to keep his head above water amongst London's unwanted flotsam and jetsam.

1. *An advertisement card for the American Exchange, where Dr Lamson tried to cash a cheque.*

Once more, George Henry Lamson's thoughts went to his crippled brother-in-law Percy Malcolm John, half of whose £3 000 fortune would go to Mrs Lamson were he to expire while still a minor. He made plans for Percy to come to the Chichester hotel during his Christmas holidays, and the lad gratefully accepted the invitation. On November 11, Dr Lamson went to the chemist's shop of Messrs Bell & Co. at No. 225 Oxford Street. Asking for some paper, he wrote a prescription for a solution of morphine and sulphate of atropine. To be subcutaneously injected 'for own use'. The shop assistant John Edward Stirling made up the solution while the Doctor waited, and after looking up Lamson's entry in the Medical Directory, he supplied it to him for two shillings and ninepence. On November 16, Dr Lamson was back with another prescription for morphine and atropine for his own use, and also five grains of pure digitaline. The shop assistant Stirling found that the shop's stock of digitaline, the active principle of the foxglove plant and a potent poison if taken in large doses, was discoloured and far from fresh. He would order some more, he said, and the Doctor left with his morphine mixture. He was back again on November 20, asking for a grain of aconitine, the active principle of the monkswood root and a very potent poison, but Stirling declined to sell it to him, asking him to call at a shop where he was better known. On November 24, Dr Lamson pawned his gold hunting watch and his case of surgical instruments at Robinson's of No. 26 Mortimer Street, to obtain some much-needed funds to the tune of £5. He then went to the chemist's shop of Messrs Allen & Hanbury, in Plough

2. *Allen & Hanbury's pharmacy in Plough Court, where Dr Lamson bought his acotinine, from E.C. Cripps,* Plough Court *(London 1927).*

3. *The interior of Allen & Hanbury's pharmacy, from
E.C. Cripps,* Plough Court *(London 1927).*

Court off Lombard Street. He asked for a piece of paper and wrote "Aconitia, 2 grains, G.H. Lamson M.D., Bournemouth, Hants." The shop assistant William Ralph Dodd looked up Lamson's name and address in the Medical Directory, before weighing up the aconitine, wrapping it up in some paper marked 'Acon, Poison' and selling it for two shillings and sixpence.[11]

Dr Lamson kept up a correspondence with his mother, who was awaiting him in Paris, for them to travel on to Florence together. The original intention was for him to join her on November 20, but he sent her a last-minute telegram that he was too ill to travel. Mrs Julia Lamson then wrote him a long letter, saying that his room had been made ready in the Lamsons' Paris flat at No. 107 Rue Chaillot, and that an especially nice dinner had been ordered. She hoped that he would be able to travel the following week, since she was keen to join her husband in

Florence. Dr Lamson wrote back in November 25, saying that he had been very ill for three days: he had suffered from peritonitis and complete stoppage of the bowels, and a surgeon friend from Charing Cross Hospital had found the situation precarious indeed, and decided to operate. After Lamson had been put under with the chloroform, the surgeon performed a laparotomy, cutting the belly open and looking round the Doctor's digestive tract to find out what was wrong. He found that there had been a dangerous volvulus or twisting of the large intestine, and resected the gangrenous part, cutting into healthy tissue and stitching the Doctor's bowels together again, before closing up the belly. Since his dexterous surgeon friend had ordered Lamson to keep to his bed after this major surgery, he was unable to travel for the present time.[12] This dramatic story cannot have contained a word of truth, however, since we know that far from lying on the operating table, Dr Lamson was busy pawning his effects and buying poison on November 24. Nor did he mention to any other person that he had just had a dangerous operation performed on him, under chloroform anaesthesia.

On November 26, George Henry Lamson wrote the following letter to James Creighton Nelson, the proprietor of the hotel where he was staying: "Dear Sir, – I have been sent for to go with as little delay as possible to the place where my wife is now staying, as my little girl is quite ill, and my wife is terribly anxious about the child, and wishes besides to change her quarters. She will come to London for a short time until I leave for the Continent myself. As I am therefore very anxious to yield to her wishes, and as it would render it impossible for me to bring her back with me if I went into the city to procure the sum I require for the journey, her account, &c., up to the present time, I venture to ask you if you would be good enough to let me have £5 until my return with her in the evening (to-day). I should be very sorry to put you to any inconvenience, but I feel certain you will do this for me, knowing my parents, &c. If I do not catch the

10.30 train from Victoria I cannot return today, as it is important that I should. I should require the sitting-room (No. 29) which my mother had while here. The bedroom I now occupy would be naturally sufficient for my wife and self, but if she wishes the child to come here as well, I should require another room for her and the nurse. I shall ask you to kindly see that a large trunk is taken out of the left luggage room at Euston station and brought here and kept in a safe place, as it contains a quantity of silver plate and household valuables, worth a considerable sum. Mrs Lamson wishes to have the plate, &c., and some music contained in the same trunk for her own use. Excuse the very bad and illegible manner I have written this note, but my eye-sight is very bad by artificial light, and I have mislaid my glasses. Apologising for venturing to ask the favour I seek from you, I am, dear sir, yours faithfully, Geo. H. Lamson (Room 30)."

But Mr Nelson was an experienced hotel-keeper, used to dodgy guests trying to borrow money and obtain various favours for nothing. Although he knew that Dr Lamson's parents were respectable people, he was far from impressed with the Doctor himself, and he did not part with any £5, nor did he make exertions to have Dr Lamson's trunk brought to the hotel.[13]

On November 29, James Creighton Nelson got yet another queer letter from George Henry Lamson: "Dr. Lamson (from room 30) begs that some one may be sent to M. Buzzard's, confectioner, &c., Oxford Street, two or three doors from the Pantheon, going towards Oxford Circus, and the following articles procured and brought here for Dr. Lamson, viz., one Dundee cake, 3s. size; 2 lbs. crystallized fruits, assorted. In these fruits the following fruits to be left out: – chinois, green or yellow, or limes, and nuts. Only the following to be sent in these fruits: – apricots (glaze, not crystallized), greengages (glaze, and only two or three of them), some small yellow plum cherries, 'brochettes', knottes, and lunnettes. A large proportion of the three last articles on the 2 lbs. as ordered is desired. Dr. Lamson would suggest that the above order be shown to the attendant at Buzzard's, as the messenger would hardly be expected to remember the whole order as above given. Dr. Lamson begs may be no delay in sending for these articles, as he wishes to take them with him to Harrow for a birthday gift, and he particularly wishes to start early so as to be back soon to prepare for leaving for the Continent in the evening. As Dr. Lamson does not know the price of the articles he has ordered, he begs they may be paid for him, and he will settle when he comes down to breakfast."

But again, the experienced hotel-keeper James Creighton Nelson did not see the point of paying the bill for one of his guests. He was beginning to suspect that Dr Lamson was hard up, and must have been hoping and praying that the impecunious Doctor would have enough money to settle his bill when he left.[14]

On November 30, Dr Lamson travelled from London to Portsmouth by train, and then on to Ryde on the Isle of Wight. The Ryde stationmaster John Henry Artridge saw him at the Ryde pierhead. Lamson told him that he was travelling on to Ventnor, where he and his family were well known, but unfortunately he had no money at all. Artridge allowed him to travel for free, in the charge of a guard. In Ventnor, the Doctor went to see an old friend of his, the wine merchant Price Owen, who cashed a cheque for £20, on the Wilts and Dorset bank. Owen knew Lamson's respectable family, who had been staying in Ventnor on and off since 1871, and believed the Doctor still possessed plenty of money. Dr Lamson travelled back post-haste, paying the train fare of two shillings and tenpence on the way. From Horsham, he sent a note to Price Owen that he had unfortunately written his cheque on the wrong bank, asking Owen not to send it on. He would soon be back in Ventnor, with his correct cheque-book in hand, to clear the matter up. But Lamson went back to London, the cheque was returned dishonoured, and Owen never saw his money again.[15]

★

On December 1, Dr Lamson wrote the following letter:

> "Nelson's Hotel, Great Portland Street
> London, December 1, 1881
>
> My Dear Percy – I had intended running down to Wimbledon to see you to-day, but I have been delayed by various matters until it is now nearly six o'clock, and by the time I should reach Blenheim House you would probably be preparing for bed. I leave for Paris and Florence to-morrow, and wish to see you before going. So I purpose to run down to your place as early as I can, for a few minutes even, if I can accomplish no more. Believe me, dear boy, your loving brother, G.H. Lamson."[16]

Later the same day, Dr Lamson chanced to meet an old friend in the City of London: William Tulloch, who worked as a clerk in an office in Moorgate Street. Both William and his medical student brother John Law Tulloch had known Lamson since 1878, and they had both attended his wedding in that year. Knowing that the Doctor was handy with his surgical knives, William Tulloch asked him to operate on an abscess in the armpit from which he had been suffering. The location where this surgical procedure took place remains unknown, but the patient was definitely grateful, since he invited Lamson for luncheon the following day.

On December 2, the two Tulloch brothers and Dr Lamson enjoyed quite a jolly meal together, at John Law Tulloch's lodgings at No. 14 Alma Square, St John's Wood. Lamson told his two friends that in the evening, he was going to Wimbledon to visit his crippled young brother-in-law, before he was off to join his father in Florence. John Law Tulloch accompanied Lamson back to Nelson's Hotel and helped him pack up his luggage for the forthcoming journey; they went to Waterloo Station in a hansom cab to deliver the Doctor's large portmanteau. The hotel-keeper

4. *A postcard showing Alma Square, where Dr Lamson visited his friend John Law Tulloch.*

5. *Tulloch's lodgings at No. 14 Alma Square as they look today.*

James Creighton Nelson was of course eager for his bill to be settled, since the Doctor had been staying at his hotel for a full month, but Lamson successfully fobbed him off, saying that he had left two other portmanteaus in his room; when he returned to fetch these the following day, he would settle the bill. Although an experienced hotel-keeper, Nelson fell for that one; since the deceitful Doctor had no intention to return to the hotel, Nelson would never see his money. Instead of going to Waterloo Station, Lamson and Tulloch took the train to Wimbledon, arriving around 6 pm. Since Blenheim House School was just a short walk away from the station, Tulloch waited at a public house as Lamson walked off towards the school.

Dr Lamson soon returned to the pub, saying that Percy was very ill, and getting worse. The headmaster Mr Bedbrook, who was a director of the South-Eastern Railway Company, had recommended him not to cross from Dover to Calais that evening, since there was a bad boat on the service. The two friends returned to central London and visited the newly constructed Royal Comedy Theatre in Panton Street, where 'The Mascotte' and 'Seeing Frou-Frou' were currently playing. They then went to a public house, where Lamson wrote a cheque for £12 10s. in Tulloch's favour. They tried to cash it at the Adelphi Hotel in Adam Street, but since the hotel landlord was wary of bad cheques and refused to cash it, they went on to the Eyre Arms in Finchley Road, where the bibulous John Law Tulloch was a regular customer. After the landlord had cashed the cheque, Tulloch handed the money over to Lamson.[17]

The mysterious movements of Dr Lamson on December 2 are worthy of a short discourse, since in fact, he went nowhere near Blenheim House School that evening. His statements to Tulloch that he had seen Percy, and spoken to Mr Bedbrook about his passage to France, were nothing but a pack of lies. Had the Doctor intended to go to the school to see Percy, but lost his courage in the last minute; had he been too short of money

6. *The Royal Comedy Theatre in Panton Street, where Dr Lamson and John Law Tulloch amused themselves after their mysterious expedition to Wimbledon on December 2, from the* Illustrated London News, *October 15 1881.*

7. *The interior of the Royal Comedy Theatre, from the* Graphic, *December 17 1881.*

8. A postcard showing the Eyre Arms as No. 1 Finchley Road, stamped and posted in 1905. The pub has long been demolished, and a mansion block today occupies the site.

9. Dr Lamson cashes a cheque with the pub landlord at the Eyre Arms, from *Famous Crimes Past & Present*.

to afford his passage to Paris; had he wanted to make a trial run before his expedition to Wimbledon the following day; or had he belatedly realized that Tulloch might prove a very inconvenient witness? This matter was never resolved.

Dr Lamson and John Law Tulloch met again the following afternoon, at the Adelphi Hotel. The Doctor seemed unusually distracted and preoccupied; he said that since he was now too late to catch the London to Paris train, they should go to the Horse Shoe public house for some refreshments. They sat swigging from their glasses for quite a while, until Lamson said that since he had now missed yet another train, he should go in the evening. They then went back to the Eyre Arms, before parting at 6 pm.[18] The Doctor went off alone, having brooded over his misfortunes, and made his terrible decision. This evening, there would be no 'trial run'. Fly the fangs of Belisarius!

V.

THE HOUR OF DEATH

On Saturday December 3 1881, Percy Malcolm John was carried downstairs to the school dining-room just as usual, to have tea, bread and butter for breakfast. The previous day, he had sat his examinations, and before luncheon, he helped another pupil revise for his own examinations the following week. Percy enjoyed a meal of stewed rabbit with onion sauce and potatoes for his luncheon, and in the afternoon took part in some charades with the other boys, wheeling himself about in his chair as well as he could. When tea was served at 5.45 pm, Percy had another meal of tea, bread and butter. Afterwards, he looked through some examination papers with another pupil named Banbury. The day before, he had told Mr Bedbrook that he was expecting his brother-in-law Dr Lamson to come visiting, and at 6.55 pm on Saturday, the Doctor did come calling. Mr Bedbrook had seen him several times before, but he still could hardly recognize him because Lamson had lost much weight.

The pupil Walter Edward Banbury carried Percy upstairs to the ground floor dining-room, which was used when the boys had visitors, and he was placed in an armchair. Dr Lamson, who knew Banbury, said "I thought you would have been in India by this time," referring to his intended passing into the army. Turning to Percy, the jovial Doctor exclaimed "Why, how fat you are looking, Percy, old boy!" "I wish I could say the same of you, George," the crippled lad replied, referring to Lamson's thin and haggard

*1. A vignette on the 'Wimbledon Mystery',
from* Famous Crimes Past & Present.

*2. The Blenheim House murder school at No. 1-2 St George's Road,
Wimbledon, from* Famous Crimes Past & Present.

looks. When Mr Bedbrook poured some glasses of sherry, and the Doctor asked for some sugar, saying that he believed that the sherry contained a large amount of brandy, and that the sugar would counteract the effect of the alcohol. Bedbrook said that he believed the opposite to be true, but he did ring the bell for a basin of sugar, which was brought by the school matron, Mrs Mary Ann Bowles. Dr Lamson put some sugar into his sherry with a spoon, stirred it with his pen-knife and took a sip. The Doctor then produced a black leather bag, from which he produced some sweets and a Dundee cake wrapped in newspaper, which he cut into slices with his pen-knife as Mr Bedbrook and Percy watched him. All three swigged from their glasses, and ate from the cake and sweets with relish, keeping up a light conversation the mean while.

Dr Lamson then said "Oh, by the way, Mr Bedbrook, when I was in America I thought of you and your boys; I thought what excellent things these capsules would be for your boys to take nauseous medicines in." He handed Bedbrook two half-empty boxes of American gelatine capsules, which he said would come in handy for giving the boys medicine. Bedbrook took an empty capsule and swallowed it. The Doctor took another capsule and filled it with sugar from the basin, saying "Before you take it, shake it like this; that will send the medicine to one end." He then exclaimed "Here, Percy, you are a swell pill-taker; take this, and show Mr Bedbrook how easily it may be swallowed!" Percy obediently took his medicine, and in one gulp it was gone.[1]

Dr Lamson next said that he must be going, to take the train to Florence via Paris, since he needed a holiday for his indifferent health. The time was around 7.20 pm and Mr Bedbrook knew that there was one train from Wimbledon to London at 7.21, and another at 7.50. He advised the Doctor to go at once, since the Wimbledon railway station was less than a minute's walk from the school. Lamson showed no urgency, however, saying an affectionate goodbye to Percy and staying for more than a

3. Percy is given a pill, from Famous Crimes Past & Present.

minute. When Mr Bedbrook was showing him out through the drawing-room, the Doctor said that he thought Percy's curvature of the spine was getting worse, meaning that the poor boy would not last much longer. A railway porter named George Lamb saw Dr Lamson come hurrying just before the 7.21 train was due, asking for the right platform for Waterloo. He quickly boarded the train, which just then came steaming in, but he must have been dissatisfied with something, since he asked Lamb whether there was sufficient time to change carriages, which there

4. A drawing of Dr Lamson, from the Penny Illustrated Paper, *March 11 1882.*

5. Wimbledon Station, from an old postcard.

only just was. The Doctor wrote something on an envelope, put some coins inside, and handed it to Lamb, asking him to take it to Blenheim House School. Strangely, this missive was intended as a last-minute 'tip' for Percy, the boy he had just left behind to face the hour of death.[2]

*

After Dr Lamson had disappeared into the dark December night, Percy remained seated in his armchair. There was a piano in

6. *Dr Lamson sends a railway porter from Wimbledon Station to Blenheim House School, from* Famous Crimes Past & Present.

the dining-room, and Mr Bedbrook was visited by two young ladies for a music lesson. Percy stayed in the room as they played and sang for about fifteen minutes. But two minutes after Mr Bedbrook had shown the two young musical students out into the drawing-room for some further education, Percy said "I feel as if I had an attack of heartburn." Mr Bedbrook, who was having a large party at the school that evening, with more than sixty people invited, went to attend to his guests, leaving Percy reading some papers Dr Lamson had brought with him.

When Mr Bedbrook returned to see Percy five minutes later, the crippled lad was clearly unwell. He said "I feel as I felt after my brother-in-law had given me a quinine pill at Shanklin." Percy wanted to go to bed, and a pupil named Joseph Bell carried him upstairs, accompanied by the pupil Banbury. Since Mr Bedbrook was busy with his party in the drawing-room, he was prevented from attending Percy himself, but the matron Mary Ann Bowles and the junior master Alfred Godward were in the sick-room. They called Mr Bedbrook when Percy suddenly got much worse. He was seized with convulsions, screamed aloud with pain, and had to be forcibly held down on the bed as he threw himself about in his agony. The startled headmaster ran downstairs when he saw the state of his wretched pupil. He knew that Dr Other Windsor Berry, the local medical practitioner, had been invited to his party, and it turned out that at 8.55 pm, the doctor had just arrived.

Mr Bedbrook showed Dr Berry upstairs, where he found Percy in a dreadful condition. Tormented by his agonies, the unfortunate lad desperately screamed 'My throat is closing!' and 'My skin is being drawn up!', retched terribly, and vomited a quantity of dark-coloured fluid. He was very restless, like if he was suffocating to death, desperately throwing himself backwards and forwards in the bed, and from side to side; it took several people to hold him down and prevent him from falling out of bed. Dr Berry asked Percy if he had ever been ill like this before, and in a groaning voice, the luckless lad replied that his brother-in-law had once given him a quinine pill when he was at Shanklin, although he had then not been as poorly as he was now. Then the invalid again started screaming and thrashing about in his bed. Dr Berry ordered some white of egg to be beaten up in water and given to the patient, and hot poultices were applied to his stomach. Dr Berry clearly had brought his black bag when visiting Mr Bedbrook at Blenheim House School, but it may well have lacked one important contraption that might prove useful in cases of suspected poisoning, namely the stomach-pump; at least, no attempt was made to evacuate the stomach contents of the suffering invalid.

It turned out that another doctor was also attending Mr Bedbrook's party, namely the local practitioner Dr Edward Stephen Little. The two doctors consulted as to the best thing to be done, before deciding to inject morphine. Since Dr Berry's medical bag did not contain a hypodermic syringe either, he had to run home to his house to fetch one. He was away for about ten minutes, before successfully injecting a quarter of a grain of morphine subcutaneously under the skin of the stomach at 10 pm. Percy's agony abated somewhat, but he grew progressively weaker. At a little before eleven, his torments were as terrible as ever, as the dying boy fought for his life in a gruesome struggle. The doctors noted that his breathing became slower and sighing, and that the action of his heart became progressively weaker. Dr Berry tried to give him some brandy and water, but the dying boy could hardly swallow it. At 11.20 pm, Percy Malcolm John was finally relieved of his sufferings, when he quietly departed this life.[3]

★

Dr Berry and Dr Little may have been ill-equipped to deal with this unexpected medical emergency, having looked forward to a pleasant evening get-together at Blenheim House School, rather than a gruesome sick-bed horror, but they were no fools. Albeit lacking formal toxicological expertise, they both suspected that some irritant poison had been administered to the luckless lad. They made sure that Percy's vomit was collected into a breakfast cup, transferred into a clean bottle from Dr Berry's surgery, and later handed over to Dr Thomas Bond, Lecturer in Forensic Medicine at Westminster Hospital, for analysis.

At 11.30 on Sunday morning, Mr Bedbrook went to the Wimbledon police station, where he gave a full account of the events of the previous night to Inspector John Fuller. Inspector Fuller went to see Dr Berry, who also volunteered a long statement about the case. At 9 pm, the Inspector came to Blenheim House School to collect the evidence. He took charge of a box half full of capsules, some cake, some sweets and crystallised fruit, and all the sugar and sherry. Mr Bedbrook had ransacked Percy's belongings and found a small medicine-chest with twenty samples of what

7. *The two doctors confront Mr Bedbrook to declare that there has been a murder, from* Famous Crimes Past & Present.

8. The gravestone of Percy Malcolm John at Wimbledon Cemetery (today Gap Road Cemetery), from Famous Crimes Past & Present.

was stated to be quinine powders, with a label saying 'D.W. Littlechild, chemist, Ventnor'. Appreciating that the suspicious death of Percy Malcolm John was mysterious indeed, Inspector Fuller communicated with Scotland Yard, and it was decided that their experienced detectives should take charge of the case. All the above-mentioned evidence was taken to Detective Inspector James Wallis Butcher, who had been assigned the case by Chief Superintendent Frederick Williamson.[4] After Mr G.H. Hull, the Coroner for the Western District of Surrey, had been informed of the suspicious death, he ordered an inquest to be held.

Since Percy Malcolm John had died late on a Saturday night, and since the Scotland Yard authorities decided to make no statement about the case, the London newspapers of Monday

December 5 struggled to obtain reliable information about the 'Mysterious Death of a Student at Wimbledon.' All the *Daily News* had to contribute was: "Mr Percy Malcolm John, 19 years of age, a student at Blenheim-house School, Wimbledon, died on Saturday night under circumstances of a suspicious character and after a visit from his brother-in-law, Mr G.F. Lamson, a surgeon in practice at Bournemouth. Mr Lamson is believed to have left London for France."[5] The *Pall Mall Gazette* added that Dr Lamson's visit had only lasted for 20 minutes or so, and that not long after he left, Percy felt ill. The facts of the case have cause for grave suspicions, and although a Central News telegram denied that the order for an arrest had been made, it did confirm that the Scotland Yard detectives were actively making inquiries.[6] An adventurous *Standard* journalist had found out, probably from either Mr Bedbrook or one of the two doctors, that Percy had mentioned a previous incident when he had been taken ill after Dr Lamson had given him a quinine pill at Shanklin. The journalist added the fiction that Percy had cried out, on his sick-bed, "That brother of mine has done for me this time!" Dr Lamson, who had left the school in a somewhat hurried and excited manner, was presumed to have caught the 7.20 train from Wimbledon to Waterloo, from whence he was likely to have proceeded to Paris. A short and dangerously erroneous description of the fugitive Doctor was provided by this newspaper: he was 35 years old and had fair hair cut close, whiskers and a moustache.[7] As we know, Lamson was in fact 29 years old, dark-haired and bearded.

On Tuesday December 6, Dr Berry and Dr Little performed the post-mortem examination of Percy Malcolm John, together with Dr Bond. With the exception of the severe scoliosis and the paralysis of his lower limbs, Percy had been a muscular and healthy-looking young man. All inner organs were in a healthy state, apart from the lungs, which had a few old adhesions. There was slight congestion of the brain, and considerable congestion of the liver, spleen and kidneys. The mucous membrane of the stomach was severely inflamed and congested, as was the first part of the duodenum; there were patches of congestion in the other parts of the small intestine. Dr Berry's impression was that Percy had died from the administration of an irritant vegetable poison. Dr Bond made sure that the stomach, slices of the liver, the gall-bladder, both kidneys and part of the spleen were taken for analysis, as were the three or four ounces of urine found in the bladder.[8]

Later the same day, the Coroner Mr George Henry Hull opened the inquest on Percy Malcolm John at the Drill Hall. Superintendent Digby and Inspector Butcher watched on behalf of the police, and the solicitor Mr T.C. Summerhays watched on behalf of Mr Bedbrook. There was great interested in the proceedings, and the room was densely crowded. After being sworn, the jurors had to walk nearly a mile to the mortuary of Wimbledon Cemetery, where Percy's mangled remains were kept in a coffin. The jurors viewed the body, and after they had reconvened, Mr Bedbrook formally identified the dead youth as his former pupil Percy Malcolm John, who would have been 19 years old on December 18; he had himself been present at the death, which had occurred at 11.30 pm on Saturday night. The Coroner said he would not take any further evidence at this early stage. He expressed his approbation that samples of Percy's inner organs had been placed in competent hands for analysis, adjourned the inquest for two weeks, and gave an order for the body to be buried.[9] On December 8, the remains of Percy Malcolm John were interred at Wimbledon Cemetery; it is sad but true that very few people were present, and that strangely and blameworthily, neither sister of the deceased attended. A simple cross marked the site of the grave, in what is today the Gap Road Cemetery.[10]

★

On December 6, the newspapers could report that the police were looking for Dr Lamson all over the country, his old haunts in Rotherfield and Bournemouth in particular. There was a newspaper rumour that Lamson had gone to Liverpool, to accept a position as ship's doctor on board a steamer from the Inman Line, and escape back to America.[11] The police still hoped that he might voluntarily come forward. Newspaper correspondents in Sussex and Bournemouth interviewed people who had known Lamson, and they could report that the suspect was a doctor of some standing, who had been awarded several medals for gallant wartime service abroad. There was much interest in the 'Wimbledon Mystery' in Bournemouth, where Lamson had been well known as a local practitioner. His activities since leaving Bournemouth in early April 1881 remained a mystery, but it was presumed that he had gone to America.[12] There were newspaper rumours that one of Dr Lamson's relations had received a letter from the fugitive Doctor, saying that when he had read about the melancholy occurrence at Wimbledon in the London newspapers, it had shocked him so profoundly that he was now lying ill himself.

The *Daily Telegraph* managed to get an interview with Mr Bedbrook, who said that Blenheim House School had a total of 53 pupils, aged between 10 and 20, not less than 22 of whom boarded on the premises. Although Percy had begun his education late in life, he had been of a most agreeable disposition, and very talented. He had spent most of his time reading and acquired a fund of knowledge that placed him at the head of the school. He had been loved by both masters and students: just before his tragic death, he had distinguished himself by taking the highest number of marks in the examination before the College of Preceptors. There had always seemed to be a warm affection between Percy and his brother-in-law Dr Lamson, who had more than once come to the school to visit him. The Doctor had often made gloomy prognostications about Percy's health, however: it was improbable that the crippled lad would live to be 21, he predicted, due to the extreme curvature of his spine, which meant that even the slightest of falls might injure him fatally. Dr Lamson had sometimes sent him medicine for Percy through the mail, but since it has disagreed with the patient, Bedbrook had discontinued the treatment. Bedbrook himself had never noticed anything seriously wrong with Percy's health, apart from his paralysis. He denied the newspaper rumours that Percy had screamed "I don't want any of your damned quinine pills such as you gave me at Shanklin! It nearly did for me there!" Nor had Lamson said "Percy, this is the way we used to take it in America to destroy the effects of alcohol" when he poured sugar into his glass of sherry.[13]

On December 8, the London newspapers could report that in addition to the rumour that Dr Lamson himself had written to his relations, there was a report that the friends of the late Percy Malcolm John had received a telegram from the Rev. Mr Lamson in Florence, stating that his son was lying ill in Paris, overcome with the tragic news of the death of his young brother-in-law.[14] There was great interest in the 'Wimbledon Mystery' all over the country. The journalists had become aware that Percy Malcolm John was heir to considerable property, and that his sister Mrs Kate Lamson would inherit half of his wealth should he die while still a minor. There was much speculation as to the whereabouts of the fugitive Dr Lamson. Was he in Paris, as suggested by the telegram from his father, or had he gone to Liverpool in order to escape to the United States? The Scotland Yard detectives were still hoping that Lamson, who was after all an educated man from a distinguished family, would come to London to give himself up voluntarily. James Creighton Nelson the hotel-keeper had alerted them to the Doctor's recent stay at his hotel, and his speedy escape without paying his bill, but although the police searched the two portmanteaus Lamson had left behind, they did not contain any object indicative of his present whereabouts.

Percy's humble belongings at Blenheim House School had also been searched by the detectives, and a medicine-chest with some suspicious-looking pills and powders had been taken for analysis. There had also been a postcard, dated December 3 1881, which Percy had intended to send to his sister Mrs Kate Lamson at 'Patey, Fangmere, near Chichester', concerning his visit on the upcoming school holidays: "Dear old Kitten, – We break up on the 20th (Tuesday). I will write and tell you by what train I am coming."

VI.

DR LAMSON AT BAY

Dr Lamson had caught the 7.21 train from Wimbledon to Waterloo, where he grabbed the effects he had deposited there and boarded the train to Paris. He arrived on December 4, having travelled all night and most of the day, and went straight to the Lamson family's Paris flat at No. 107 Rue de Chaillot. He eagerly read the London newspapers on December 5, containing the vague early reports of the 'Suspicious Death in Wimbledon': it was clear to him that Percy was dead, and he himself a fugitive. And indeed, when he came back to the flat, a telegram just arrived, from his remaining brother-in-law William Greenhill Chapman, announcing that Percy was indeed dead. The Doctor went to send two telegrams, to his father in Florence and his brother-in-law in London:

> "Lamson Père, Pasteur à Florence, Paris 5 Dec 1881 (7 pm), Demanded in London, Percy dead, please give advice"

and

> "Chapman 29 Nicoll Road Harlesden, Doctor forbids George moving too ill prostrated by telegram"[1]

Having secured a respite for a few days, the gloomy Dr Lamson pondered his chances, sitting alone in the Paris flat. Should he

He took the paper.

1. Dr Lamson reads about himself in the newspapers, from Famous Crimes Past & Present.

2. Rue de Chaillot in Paris, where the Lamsons had their flat, from an old postcard.

travel on to Florence, as he had originally had planned, to join his father, whose advice he greatly valued? Or should he hide in Paris for a while? After all, since he knew perfect French, he could mingle with the Paris crowds, in a city he knew well since his student days. Or should he return to London to face the music? There were three problems, however. Firstly, in spite of the gullible Price Owen contributing £20 to the Doctor's purse, and his successful dodging of the London hotel bill, his travel and expenses had meant that he was now once more penniless and without any income. Secondly, if he absconded he would be searched for by a police force known for its dogged determination, and although Mrs Lamson would inherit her brother, the Doctor himself would not have his share in the spoils. Thirdly, due to a limited supply of morphine, Lamson's hypochondriasis had returned with a vengeance, and he was convinced that he was a dying man, well-nigh incapable of further travel.

On the morning of December 7, Dr Lamson purchased the *Evening Standard* newspaper of the previous day, from a Parisian newspaper stall, to read about himself. Since the report of the suspicions against himself was a good deal more accusatory than the vague hints in the papers of December 5, the gloomy Doctor returned to the Lamson flat to write a letter to his brother-in-law William Greenhill Chapman:

"Paris, Wednesday Morning, December 7, 1881.

My Dear Will, – Your letter reached me on Monday night too late to catch any train except one, *via* Dieppe, and which I should have had to rush for. This the doctor would not allow me to do. I was so prostrate at the sudden, awful, and most unexpected news that I became delirious very soon. I was obliged to remain in bed all day yesterday. Early this morning I saw the *Evening Standard*. I read therein the dreadful suspicion attached to my name. I need not tell you of the absolute falsity of such a fearful accusation. Bedbrook was present all the time I was in the house, and if there was any noxious substance in the capsule it must have been in his sugar, for that was all that was in it. He saw me take the empty capsule and fill it from his own sugar basin. However, with the consciousness that I am an innocent and unjustly accused man, I am returning at once to London to face the matter out. If they wish to arrest me they will have ample opportunity of doing so. I shall attempt no concealment. I shall arrive at Waterloo station about 9.15 tomorrow (Thursday) morning. Do try and meet me there. If I do not see you there I shall go straight to your house, trusting to the possibility of finding Kitty there. In great haste, yours truly, Geo. H. Lamson."[2]

This letter clearly indicates that after a few days of pondering, Dr Lamson had made up his mind to return to London. It is also instructive that he felt a need to explain the happenings at Blenheim House School to his brother-in-law, to draw attention away from the capsule Percy had been given, which had been considered indicative of deliberate poisoning in the early newspaper accounts, and present his own version of events, inculpating Mr Bedbrook in the process. Whereas the trusting Mrs Lamson, or 'Kitty' as she was known, could be relied upon to do what she was told by her husband, William Greenhill Chapman was less likely to be impressed by his arguments. Chapman had known Percy well, having been a witness when Dr Lamson had given him a suspicious pill at Shanklin, causing sickness and diarrhoea. If the Doctor distrusted Chapman, his suspicions were well-founded, since his brother-in-law did in fact make haste to contact the police: in the evening of December 7, Detective Inspector James Wallis Butcher came to call, inspecting Dr Lamson's letter from Paris with great interest. Not trusting the Doctor's intention to turn himself in, he sent Detective Sergeant Moser to Paris the following day, to seek out Lamson at the family flat.

For once, Dr Lamson turned out to be as good as his word, however. He had a mishap with his connection and sent Chapman a telegram: "Boat too late for early train, shall therefore only arrive at Waterloo about 10.30. Please meet me as by letter." After a day and a night of travelling, he alighted at Waterloo at 10.30 am. In spite of the Doctor's exhortations, William Greenhill Chapman was not there to meet him, but Mrs Lamson, who had been staying with Chapman in London, had come to meet her darling husband, of whose complete innocence she was convinced. After a brief conference with his wife, the gloomy Doctor went straight to Scotland Yard, where he asked for Detective Inspector Butcher, whose name he had seen in the *Evening Standard* as that of the officer in charge of the investigation of the 'Wimbledon Mystery'. The sergeant

3. Old Scotland Yard, from Vol. 3 of Hargrave L. Adam's Police Encyclopaedia.

on duty asked the two Lamsons to wait in a small interrogation room. When Inspector Butcher entered the room, Dr Lamson asked to confirm his identity. Then the Doctor said "My name is Lamson; I am Dr Lamson, whose name has been mentioned in connection with the death at Wimbledon." Somewhat taken aback that the fugitive Doctor had returned to London after all, Butcher asked him to be seated. "I have called to see what is to be done about it; I considered it best to do so; I read the account in the public papers in Paris, and came over this morning; I have only just arrived in London; I am very unwell and much upset about this matter, and am not in a fit state at all to have undertaken the journey." Surprised that the Doctor was speaking of the tragic death of his brother-in-law like if it had been some trivial misunderstanding, Butcher sent a message to alert Chief Superintendent Williamson. He told Lamson that he would have to remain at Scotland Yard for some time.

4. A caricature of Superintendent Williamson, from Punch, April 21 1883.

Mrs Lamson had come with her husband to Scotland Yard, and she made light conversation with him as they waited for the Chief Superintendent to make himself known. Finally, Dr Lamson said "Where is the delay? I thought I would come here and leave my address. I am going into the country, to Chichester, so that you would know where to find me and attend the inquest. I have travelled from Paris *via* Havre and Southampton; I went over *via* Dover and Calais." Butcher then went out to see Chief Superintendent Williamson, who told him that Lamson must not be allowed to leave Scotland Yard. Detective Inspector Butcher called Lamson into another room and said "Your case has been fully considered, and it has been decided to charge you with causing the death of Percy John. I thereupon take you into custody, and charge you with causing the death of Percy Malcolm John at Blenheim House, Wimbledon, on 3rd December." Looking quite disappointed, the Doctor said "Very well. Do you think bail will

5. *Mrs Lamson protests her husband's innocence, from* Famous Crimes Past & Present.

be accepted? I hope the matter will be kept as quiet as possible for the sake of my relations." The distraught Mrs Lamson tried to shield the Doctor from the two detectives, dramatically crying out "Before Heaven, my husband is innocent!"

Detective Inspector Butcher said that he was going to convey Dr Lamson to the Wandsworth Police Court in a cab, since the question of bail rested with the magistrates. On the way, they stopped at the Wandsworth police station for Lamson to be formally searched. In his pockets, Inspector Butcher found two letters, one signed 'J.W.L.' and the other 'W. Tulloch', an envelope containing the Doctor's Paris address, a pawnbroker's ticket for a case of surgical instruments and a gold watch, a cloak-room ticket from the North-Western Railway, a cheque-book upon the Bournemouth branch of the Wilts and Dorset Bank, seven and a half francs and six and a half pence in bronze, and a small pocket diary. The cloak-room ticket led the detectives to a box at Euston Station, containing some prescription-books, some sheet-music, a pile of silver plate, and a quantity of letters.[3]

★

Later the same day, Dr Lamson was taken before the Wandsworth police court, where the veteran magistrate Mr John Paget was presiding. Lamson was described as "a well-dressed and gentlemanly-looking man of about 5ft 8in in height. He wore a moustache and beard, the latter cut rather close to the chin, and was attired in a well-fitting frock coat."[4] Another newspaper said that the Doctor was "a medium-sized man, apparently about 35 years of age, rather spare built, with close-cropped thick dark beard and moustache. He looked pale and ill, but appeared perfectly self-possessed. He wore in the lapel of his coat the red button of the Legion of Honour."[5]

Mr St. John Wontner conducted the prosecution, and Chief Superintendent Williamson watched on behalf of the police. Mr

Bedbrook, the first witness, told the story of Dr Lamson's visit to his school on December 3, and the lamentable death of Percy Malcolm John not long after, as previously related in this book. Mr Wontner had no questions for him, but Dr Lamson rose up, saying that he had a few questions to ask. Since Percy had been excited about sitting his examinations on Thursday and Friday, Mr Bedbrook had expressed himself to be pleased that Lamson had come on Saturday rather than on Friday. When Bedbrook admitted that Dr Lamson had once sent him a letter saying that he was deeply anxious about the curvature of Percy's spine, the Doctor exclaimed, as sharp as a needle, "I wish a note to be taken of that!" The Clerk assured him that the answer had been taken down.

Questioned by Dr Lamson, Mr Bedbrook denied that Percy had used to complain about indigestion or constipation. He could not remember why Lamson had put sugar into the capsule, or if the intention was to prevent it from collapsing. Nor could he be sure that the capsule filled with sugar was the one swallowed by Percy. Shortly after Dr Lamson had left, a railway porter had come to the school with an envelope addressed to Percy, containing a handwritten note from Lamson, as well as a crown and a florin, clearly intended as a 'tip' for the luckless lad. Bedbrook had opened the letter and placed it on the table in front of Percy. It had since been lost, and Dr Lamson said that he would consider it a personal favour if Mr Bedbrook would search for it.

Dr Lamson next asked Mr Bedbrook who had handed over the glass of sherry from which Percy had drunk, and the exact nature of its contents, but without being able to shake the schoolmaster's evidence. He also pressed Bedbrook with regard to a letter he had sent to the school from America, containing some pills supposed to be beneficial for Percy's spine, inquiring whether these had been administered as directed. Bedbrook replied that he had indeed given Percy one of the pills, but since the lad had felt unwell after taking it, he had thrown the remainder away. Dr Other Windsor Berry next gave evidence, stating that the symptoms and post-mortem findings were consistent with the ingestion of a vegetable irritant poison. Questioned by Dr Lamson, he had never before encountered a case of poisoning with a vegetable irritant. Nor did he know whether Percy had perhaps taken an interest in chemistry, or if he had access to a stockpile of drugs and chemicals. This concluded the evidence, and Mr Paget remanded the prisoner and refused an application for bail.[6]

Dr Lamson seemed quite distraught at being refused bail, and facing prison as a consequence. When he was led into his cell by the warders, he entirely lost his composure and screamed 'I will go mad!' in a terrible voice. He was later removed to the Clerkenwell House of Corrections, where he was permitted to send a telegram to the Rev. Mr Lamson in Florence, asking his father to come to London as quickly as he could.[7]

★

6. *Dr Lamson, and some vignettes from his career, including Percy Malcolm John in his wheelchair, from the* Illustrated Police News, *March 11 1882.*

After the close of business at the Wandsworth police court on December 9, the barrister Mr Gladstone, who had been instructed by Dr Lamson's solicitor Mr Arthur Walter Mills, applied to Mr Paget to admit the Doctor to bail, on the grounds that he was in an indifferent state of health, and that he had willingly surrendered himself at Scotland Yard, where there was no warrant or charge against him. Dr Lamson's father, who was currently in Florence, was expected in London, and would be able to provide bail, he assured the magistrate. But Mr Paget was not at all disposed to admit bail, due to the very serious charge against Lamson, to the effect that he did kill and murder Percy Malcolm John, and Mr Gladstone had to return empty-handed from his expedition to Wandsworth. As Dr Lamson sat shivering in his cell, alone and unbefriended, and imagining that he was the victim of every disease known to man, things were looking gloomy indeed for him, as the machinery of justice relentlessly ground on. There was much interest in the Lamson case all over the country, in Ventnor and Shanklin in particular, since the Lamson and John families were well known there. A Shanklin correspondent of the *Daily News* could report that Mrs Joliffe, the landlady of 'Clarence Villa' where Percy had stayed with the Chapmans, had made a statement that after Dr Lamson had come calling, she had found Percy on the floor in an apparently dying condition.[8]

On December 17, the examination of George Henry Lamson continued at the Wandsworth police court, with Mr Paget once more presiding. According to a *Pall Mall Gazette* journalist, Dr Lamson had seemed in excellent spirits when he arrived, carrying a medical textbook in his hand and bowing courteously to all the officials he passed.[9] Mr St. John Wontner appeared on behalf of the Public Prosecutor, and Mr Gladstone represented the prisoner. Quoting Taylor's *Medical Jurisprudence* regarding a case that had occurred in Germany, Mr Gladstone urged that part of the intestines of the deceased might be submitted for independent analysis, but Mr Paget said that he had no power in that matter, and could only refer him to the Home Office. Mr Wontner then addressed the court at length, outlining his case. He would prove that Mrs Lamson, wife of the prisoner and sister of the deceased, would inherit a large sum of money upon the death of Percy Malcolm John before he reached his majority. He would also prove that in the weeks prior to the murder, the prisoner had been going about trying to cash worthless cheques, and that he had been unable to pay his hotel bill. He suspected that the reason why Lamson had not visited the school to give Percy some 'medicine' on December 2, as he had originally planned, was that he lacked the money for a train ticket to Paris, a problem he was able to solve thanks to the generous landlord of the Eyre Arms, who cashed one of his worthless cheques. He would also prove that prior to the murder, Dr Lamson had purchased a quantity of the aconitine poison at Messrs Hanbury, the chemists, of Lombard Street. Lamson was listed in the Medical Directory as a doctor practicing in Bournemouth, a Licentiate of the Royal College of Physicians of Edinburgh, and possessing, among other appointments, that of surgeon to the secret police of Paris. A hotel porter named Amore would testify that during his stay at Nelson's Hotel, Lamson had been in possession of a bottle labelled 'Poison'. Mr Wontner called only one witness that day, namely the police surgeon Dr Bond, who had participated in the post-mortem examination; he had seen many cases of poisoning,

7. *More vignettes on the Lamson case, from the* Illustrated Police News, *December 24 1881.*

he declared, and from his own observations, he believed that Percy Malcolm John had been poisoned.[10]

The Rev. Mr Lamson, who had arrived in London by this time, had to take responsibility with regard to employing a first-rate defence team for his son. His choice of a barrister was the celebrated Mr Montagu Williams, who was 46 years old at the time, and at the peak of his powers. 'Monty' Williams had become a teacher of Classics at a grammar school in Ipswich as a young man, but he soon tired of this dull existence and became a militia officer instead, hoping to fight in the Crimean War but arriving too late for Sebastopol. He then became an actor for a while, before taking his professional life more seriously and reading for the Bar. He had commenced his legal practice in 1862, prosecuting the fraudster Madame Rachel, and defending the murder suspects Catherine Wilson, Henri de Tourville and Percy Lefroy Mapleton.[11] In 1866, when Bill Smith stood trial for the Cannon Street Murder of Mrs Sarah Millson, the painstaking work of Montagu Williams was instrumental in saving his life and preventing a serious miscarriage of justice.[12]

★

On December 20, Mr Hull the coroner resumed the adjourned inquest on Percy Malcolm John. Mr Wontner and Inspector Butcher were both present, and the solicitor Mr Mills watched on behalf of the accused. Mr Hull had received a letter from Dr Thomas Stephenson, the celebrated analyst from Guy's Hospital, to the effect that he and his colleague Dr Auguste Dupré were busy making the analysis of Percy's vomit and stomach contents. He had applied for a licence to experiment on animals, something he considered absolutely necessary for a satisfactory conclusion to be made. There ought to be adjournment for a fortnight, he suggested, for these experiments to be completed. Mr Hull and his jurymen extended this period of time until January 10, when the inquest would reconvene. Mr Wontner added that he was prosecuting Dr Lamson before the Wandsworth magistrate, and that he was planning to call many witnesses, the evidence from whom would be most material to the coroner's inquest.[13] Dr Anna Kingsford, the celebrated lady anti-vivisectionist, wrote to the *Daily News* to object to Dr Stephenson's planned experiments on animals, but the magistrate and coroner did not share her concerns for the hapless laboratory rodents.[14]

On December 22, George Henry Lamson was again brought up before Mr Paget at the Wandsworth police court. This time, the peppery Montagu Williams was present to harry the prosecution witnesses brought by Mr Wontner. The first of them was Dr Little, who described his visit to Mr Bedbrook at Blenheim House School, during which he had been called in to attend poor Percy on his sick-bed. He agreed with Dr Berry that the symptoms and autopsy findings indicated that the cause of death was the ingestion of a vegetable irritant poison. When Montagu Williams stood up to ask what experience this humble Wimbledon practitioner had of poisons, the doctor calmly answered "I have had no experience of poisoning, but have my opinion upon the general information I have derived from works on the subject." The next two witnesses were William Ralph Dodd and Charles Ernest Betts, the two assistants from Allen & Hanbury's pharmacy in Plough Court. Unfortunately for Dr Lamson, these two were young and alert, with memories in good working order: they could clearly identify the Doctor as the man who had come to the pharmacy about a month earlier, and bought two grains of aconitine. Dodd had wanted to put the poison in a small bottle, but Lamson had preferred to have it wrapped in paper. Montagu Williams made much of the fact that the pharmacy had no central ledger for the sale of poison to medical practitioners. And was it not careless to sell strong poison to an individual coming in from the street claiming to be a doctor, and giving a name from the Medical Directory? He was unable to

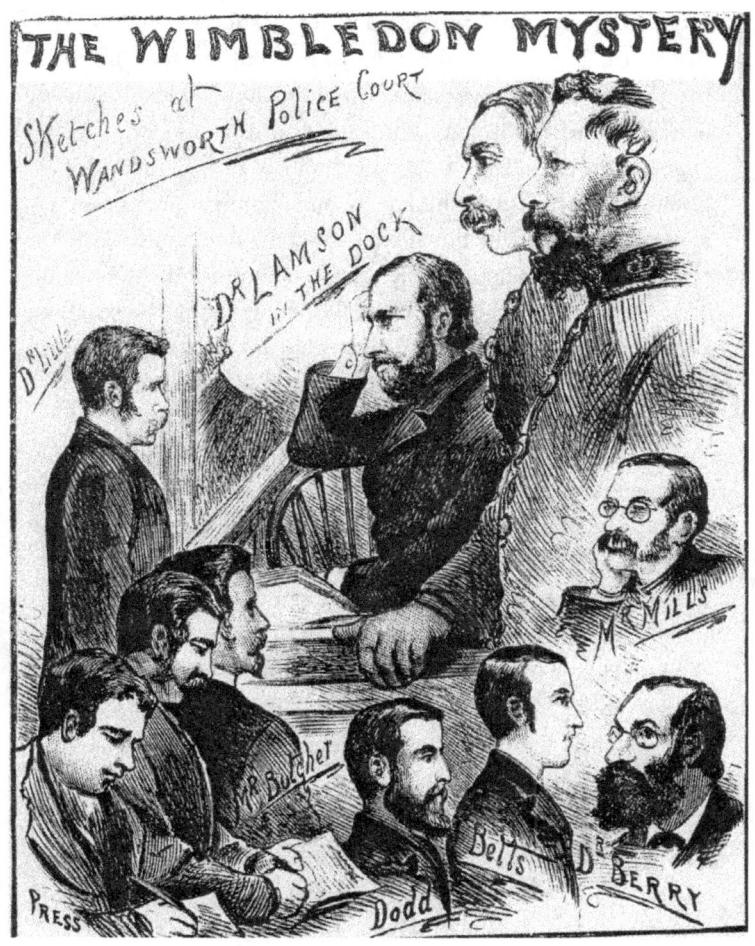

8. *Dr Lamson at the Wandsworth Police Court, from the* Illustrated Police News, *December 31 1881.*

shake these two witnesses as to their identification of Dr Lamson, however.[15]

On Christmas Eve, the Rev. Mr Lamson had a letter published in the *Times* and the *Daily News*, which is worth giving in full:

"Sir, – It is with no commonplace deprecation of judgment that I ask permission through your columns to remind the public that in the case of my son, Dr. Lamson, now detained under suspicion of foul crime, every word of explanation of defence has, under advice, been withheld. I bow to the majesty of the law as our common protection; it must do its office; but if that office carries its cold and relentless machinery roughly over hearts tenderly alive to moral reproach and to natural affection, it would be some slight assuagement of their unutterable anguish to feel that the functions of the law were moving in an atmosphere of that divine charity which believeth all things and hopeth all things in forbearance or slowness of judgment, until hope and belief should become impossible.

Surely, between the errors and mistakes of a young man oppressed with illness, suffering himself needlessly to be momentarily hampered by money embarrassments, which a single word to those who loved him would have removed, and the commission of a fearful crime upon a lad whom he had ever tenderly cared for, there is a moral distance almost infinite, and suggesting a field of charitable supposition not less great. On his way to those whom he knew would discover and relieve his troubles it can only be legally conceivable that he could turn aside for pitiful ends to the commission of the crime of which he stands accused, and bear so criminal a conscience into the presence of those with whom he was to dwell.

I am not arguing his defence, but, with a father's right and parent's sorrow, stating simply the glaring moral improbabilities of the charge, sure of that sympathetic appreciation which would check all premature judgment and prove that mercy and righteousness are ever joined in the truer movements of our nature. Yours obediently, W.O. Lamson."[16]

On December 29, Dr Lamson was brought up before the Wandsworth police court for the fourth and final time. Mr Paget could announce that due to time constraints, he had applied to the Bow Street police court to have future proceedings removed there, before Sir James Ingham in the Second Court. Both Mr Wontner and Montagu Williams expressed themselves satisfied with this arrangement. The first witness was John Edward Stirling, assistant at John Bell & Co.'s chemist's shop at No. 225 Oxford Street. Another young and alert witness, with an excellent memory, he could well remember Dr Lamson calling at the shop, asking for a mixture of morphine and atropine for his own use, and also the poisons digitaline and aconitine. Stirling had declined to sell him any aconitine, since he was not known at the shop. The next witness was Mr David Ormond, of South Norwood, the trustee under the will of Mrs Eliza John. He explained the genealogy of the John family, pointing out that after the deaths

9. *What appears to be a small print about the 'Wimbledon Mystery'.*

of Sidney and Hubert John, Percy had been the only remaining brother. Percy's money had been invested by Mr Ormond, who declared that the deceased had been good for £1 191 5s. 11d. in the London 4 per Cents and £1 078 16s. 7d. in Consols, money that was to be divided between Mrs Lamson and Mrs Chapman if he were to die while still a minor. William Greenhill Chapman was the next witness. He told the court what he knew of Dr Lamson's precedents, in particular the dramatic incident at Shanklin in late August 1881, when Percy was afflicted with severe sickness after a visit from the Doctor. After Percy's death, Chapman had telegraphed to Mrs Kate Lamson in Chichester, and the Rev. Mr Lamson in Florence. All Montagu Williams could accomplish was to expose that instead of meeting Lamson at Waterloo like a loyal brother-in-law, Chapman had called in the police and given them the Doctor's confidential letter, which gave away his address in Paris.[17]

VII.

DR LAMSON AT BOW STREET

On December 29, George Henry Lamson was brought up to the Second Court at Bow Street, before Sir James Ingham. He was described by a *Pall Mall Gazette* journalist as "a dark-complexioned man, of apparently thirty-five or forty years of age, of average height, and rather slight build."[1] A *Daily Telegraph* reporter described him as "A man of verging upon the middle age, of a sallow complexion, with a moustache and beard that had allowed to run of late a little wild, dark hair, of slight stature, clothed in a rusty suit of black, and wearing such shoes, socks and necktie as to indicate a certain impecuniosity – such was the principal actor in the scene at the court."[2] Since Dr Lamson looked feeble and ill, he was allowed to be seated in the dock. Since the Second Court, which was normally used for extradition proceedings, was not very large, the seats were all taken by the numerous journalists. The first witness was Dr Little, who was recalled to say that although he and Dr Berry had been collecting Percy's vomit from the floor with a spoon, the majority of it had been collected in a basin. John Law Tulloch then described his movements with Dr Lamson on December 2 and 3 in some detail. James Creighton Nelson said that Dr Lamson had been staying at his hotel for several weeks, before successfully dodging his bill when he left. The two letters from the Doctor, regarding his trunk deposited at Euston Station, and the purchase of sweets and a Dundee cake from a confectioner, were read at length. William

1. The Bow Street police court, from Vol. 1 of Hargrave L. Adam's Police Encyclopaedia.

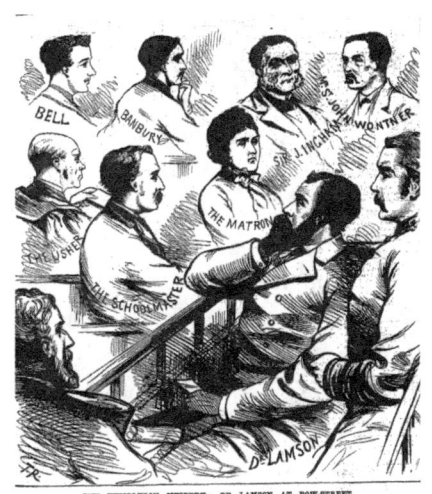

2. Dr Lamson at Bow Street, from the Penny Illustrated Paper, *January 7 1882.*

3. Last sketches of Dr Lamson at Bow Street, from the Penny Illustrated Paper, *January 14 1882.*

Amour, head porter at Nelson's Hotel, could well remember that both Dr Lamson and his parents had stayed at the hotel in the past. When he had helped to pack up Lamson's effects, he had noticed a small blue bottle marked 'poison', which he had been instructed put inside the portmanteau the Doctor brought with him when he absconded from the hotel. Amour had been much dismayed when the deceitful Doctor had not returned to pay his bill, preferring to leave behind the two heavy portmanteaus he had filled with various junk.

Sydney Herbert, cashier at the American Exchange, who knew Dr Lamson by sight, testified that on November 28, the Doctor had come sauntering in, introducing himself as the son of the Rev. Mr Lamson. He had tried to cash a cheque for £15, but since Herbert's supervisor was out, and since as a Londoner he was wary of bad cheques, he had declined to carry out this transaction. The American Exchange had later received a damaged parcel addressed to Dr Lamson, containing a box of capsules of American manufacture. William Tulloch then described Dr Lamson's successful operation on his abscess, after the completion of which the two friends had partaken of some cake and crystallised fruits. After the Wimbledon Station porter George Lamb had given an account of how Dr Lamson had boarded his train and left behind a macabre last-minute 'tip' for poor Percy, which Lamb had dutifully delivered at Blenheim House School, the day's business was concluded.[3] The newspaper report of the magisterial examination in the *Morning Post* had an odd and inexplicable postscript: "For several days past detectives have been engaged in the Isle of Wight in connection with the charge preferred against Dr. G. H. Lamson. It is reported that the authorities contemplate having the body of Herbert John, the brother of the late Percy Malcolm John, exhumed. He died at Ventnor suddenly in 1870, and was interred at Bonchurch. The case has created considerable interest in the Isle of Wight, where Dr. Lamson and his family, as well as the family of the deceased, are well known." But we know that Hubert William John (so spelt) in fact died in Dr Lamson's house, Horse Grove in Rotherfield, in June 1879 (thus not 1870); that he was buried at Bonchurch, a village to the east of Ventnor, is possible but entirely unproven.[4]

On January 2 1882, George Henry Lamson was again brought up before Sir James Ingham at Bow Street. The first witness was the recalled William Henry Bedbrook. He denied ever having been director of any railway company, and declared that there was no foundation at all for Dr Lamson's statement to that effect. Percy had studied chemistry at the school the previous term, but not the term when he died; although acids were kept on the premises, the pupils could not get their hands on them without Mr Bedbrook's permission. Bedbrook had once received a box of pills from America, along with a letter from Dr Lamson that expressed anxiety for his young brother-in-law's health, and a desire that the pills should be made use of for the benefit of Percy's spine. Cross-examined by Montagu Williams, Mr Bedbrook could not explain why only two of the original twelve pills were left in the box; the letter from Lamson was no longer in existence, and the headmaster thought he might have destroyed it.

The pupils Bell and Banbury next gave evidence describing their experiences the evening Percy expired; the latter added that when, in the summer of 1880, he had visited Dr Lamson in Bournemouth, the Doctor had made use of his usual gloomy prognostications, saying that Percy would not live much longer. Mrs Mary Ann Bowles, the matron at Blenheim House School, then described how she had provided Dr Lamson with some sugar for his sherry on December 3. She had seen the box of pills sent from America for Percy's alleged benefit, and Percy had shown her the letter Lamson had sent him from Nelson's Hotel on December 1. The classics master Alexander Watt and the assistant master Alfred Godward both thought Percy had been in his usual health and spirits on December 3, prior to the visit from Dr Lamson.

Inspector James Wallis Butcher, of the detective police, next described how he had learnt of the suspicious death of Percy Malcolm John when Inspector Fuller had handed the case over to Scotland Yard, and how the vital evidence from Blenheim House School had been secured and sent for analysis. He described his detective work, visiting Nelson's Hotel and the American Exchange, and seeking out the assistants Betts and Dodd at the Plough Court pharmacy. A number of letters had been confiscated from the portmanteaus Dr Lamson had left behind at the hotel, some of them interesting enough to be read out loud in court. Before marrying Kate George John, the sneaky Dr Lamson had written to the aforementioned trustee Mr David Ormond, in order to find out more about his future bride's potential as an heiress; he had carefully preserved the rather non-committal reply to his letter. A disagreeable letter from Dr W. Frazer M.D., Hon. Secretary of the Bournemouth Medical Society, announced the Doctor's unceremonious expulsion from this society. There was also a letter from the trusting editor William Stevenson, who had done what he could to help Dr Lamson after the bailiffs had come to call: at the executive auction of the effects seized at 'Hursley', he had bought Lamson's horse, morning chair and secretaire, and also a box of Mrs Lamson's effects that he had been gallant enough to forward to her. In his letter, Stevenson alluded to two other people Dr Lamson owed money, the father of one of whom was threatening an indictment of the Doctor on a charge of fraud, for falsifying his books.[5] The session ended with the pawnbroker Thomas Alfred Robinson identifying Dr Lamson as the person who had pledged a watch and a case of surgical instruments in his shop.

★

On January 6, George Henry Lamson was again brought up before Sir James Ingham at Bow Street. As the *Daily News* expressed it, "the interest in this case continues to grow, to judge from the largely increased number of persons who seek to gain admission to the court. Several gentlemen were yesterday accommodated with seats on the magistrates' bench, and the body of the court was completely filled with spectators." The first witness was the Ventnor chemist Charles Albert Smith, who had sold atropine and aconitine to Dr Lamson, before Percy was given some medicine at Shanklin back in late August 1881, and the Doctor made a hurried departure to America. Mrs Maria Joliffe, of Clarence Villa, Shanklin, identified herself as the landlady of William Greenhill Chapman and his wife. She had been present when Percy had fallen ill after Dr Lamson had come to visit in September 1881. The luckless lad had complained of feeling strange all over, like if he was going to be paralysed. The following morning, she had risen at 6 am. When Percy rang the bell, she could see, from the copious contents of his chamber-pot, that he had been 'very much relaxed' during the night. After Mrs Joliffe had given Percy a cup of tea and some victuals, the invalid gradually recovered during the day.

James W. Littlefield, a pharmaceutical chemist at No. 96 High Street, Ventnor, testified that he knew Dr Lamson, and had sold him various chemicals over the years, including the box of quinine powders found among Percy's belongings. The

4. *A caricature of Sir James Ingham, from* Punch, *May 12 1883.*

Doctor Poison

ANOTHER FACT.

Sister Mary.—GRANDMAMA, DOLLY MUST NOT STAY AND LISTEN TO THIS ABOUT DR. LAMSON; SHE WILL BE FRIGHTENED AT NIGHT!
Grandmama.—OF COURSE NOT. DOLLY, GO AND PLAY WITH THE PARROT. *Dolly.*—MUST I? I DON'T THINK IT WILL HURT. THEY LET ME STAY IN THE ROOM AT HOME WHEN THEY ARE READING ABOUT MR GLADSTONE

stationmaster Artridge and the wine merchant Price Owen then described the Doctor's flying visit to Ventnor on November 30, cashing a bad cheque and leaving with £20. Meyrick Heath, cashier at the Bournemouth branch of the Wilts and Dorset Banking Company, gave details of Dr Lamson's overdrawn bank account. After Inspector John Fuller other senior policemen had described delivering samples of Percy's inner organs, and specimens of his vomit, Dr Thomas Stevenson introduced himself as a doctor of medicine, a Fellow of the Royal College of Physicians, and a lecturer on chemistry and medical jurisprudence at Guy's Hospital. He had more than ten years of experience of cases of suspected poisoning. With his colleague Dr Dupré, of Westminster Hospital, he had been instructed by the Home Office to investigate the cause of death of Percy Malcolm John.

Dr Stevenson described how Dr Bond had delivered a quantity of glass bottles, containing Percy's liver, spleen and kidneys, the entire stomach, parts of the large and small bowels, the stomach contents and vomit, a quantity of wafers, and a box containing two pills wrapped in tinfoil. He had made extractions from the organs, and from the stomach contents and vomit. In the extracts, he noted the presence of an alkaloidal substance, which he tasted on his tongue and found indistinguishable from aconitine. He injected some of the extract subcutaneously into the back of a mouse, which soon showed signs of being poisoned, and died within a quarter of an hour. One of the pills found inside Percy's medicine-chest was partitioned and an extraction performed; this extract also tasted exactly like aconitine, and an experiment on a mouse had an equally fatal ending. After the evidence of Dr Bond and Dr Berry had been read aloud in court, Dr Stevenson concluded that he agreed with Dr Bond that Percy had died from being poisoned. He added that in his opinion, the poison had not been a local irritant, but the vegetable alkaloid aconitine; it would have been enough to place a minute amount of this potent poison inside the capsule swallowed by Percy to death to ensue.

Having taken in Dr Stevenson's very damning evidence against his client, Montagu Williams said that he would not make any comments at the present time, since the coroner's inquest on Percy Malcolm John was not yet concluded, and since he had no doubt that Dr Lamson would be committed for trial. When Sir James Ingham asked Dr Lamson whether he had anything to say for himself, the defiant Doctor firmly exclaimed "I merely wish to say that I am not guilty, but, by the advice of my counsel, I reserve my defence." Sir James then remanded him in custody until January 19, when he would be brought up and formally committed to stand trial for murder at the Old Bailey.[6]

★

As the machinery of justice ground slowly on, the coroner's inquest on Percy Malcolm John was resumed at the Drill Hall on January 10. Mr Bedbrook, the first witness, described how Percy had been taken to his school by Mr and Mrs Chapman, and installed there for the foreseeable future, until the Doctor came calling to give him some 'medicine'. Dr Berry and Dr Bond gave evidence, as did Mrs Bowles the matron and the pupils Walter Banbury and Joseph Bell. The latter claimed to have heard Percy scream, in his agony, "Damn that brother-in-law of mine, he has done for me!" Bank cashiers and pharmacists went on to give evidence, until Mr Hull the coroner adjourned the inquest until Friday January 13.

As the inquest resumed, Dr Thomas Stevenson and his colleague Dr Auguste Dupré gave evidence. Questioned by a juryman, Dr Stevenson said that one sixteenth of a grain of aconitine would probably cause death, and one tenth of a grain would be certain to do so. Since there had been enough aconitine in the urine to be detected by analysis, he believed that Percy had taken more than a grain of this poison. In three out of a dozen quinine powders examined, there had been enough poison to destroy the life of an adult person, and the pills Dr Lamson had sent to Percy had also contained aconitine. It was fortunate for the accident-prone lad that Mr Bedbrook had recommended him to put these pills and powders away in his medicine-chest and not make any further experiments taking them.

The foreman of the jury then suggested to the coroner that they had heard enough evidence for their minds to be made up. Mr Hull made a brief summing-up, pointing out that through his wife, Dr Lamson would have obtained money from the death of Percy Malcolm John. After attempting to murder the boy by sending him poison through the mail, there was reason to believe that the Doctor had come to the school in person to make sure Percy took his 'medicine'. Dr Lamson had purchased two grains of aconitine beforehand, and it was likely that he had given most, if not all, of this poison to Percy in the capsule. The foreman asked the jurors if they wanted to retire, but they declined, returning a verdict of wilful murder against George Henry Lamson. They expressed their sympathy with Mr Bedbrook, and their regret that such a sad event would have occurred in the school he had conducted.

On the morning of January 19, Dr Lamson was brought up before Sir James Ingham at Bow Street. Some people had come to see him as a curiosity, and the socialite Mr Burnaby, Lady St Leonards and Lady Edward Spencer Churchill occupied seats on the bench. Dr Lamson appeared thoughtful and self-occupied as he was formally committed to stand trial for murder at the Old Bailey. The plan was to deal with the Lamson case with some expedition, and the Grand Jury returned a true bill for the trial to go ahead. Montagu Williams wanted the trial to be postponed, however, for him to have the time to scrutinize the medical evidence. He gave notice to the Solicitor-General, Sir Farrer Herschell, who would lead the prosecution, that he wanted the trial to be postponed until the next sessions, since the case was a complicated one, and involved a large mass of evidence. When Dr Lamson was placed at the bar of the Old Bailey on February 1, to plead to the indictment charging him with the wilful murder of Percy Malcolm John, Montagu Williams argued that it was absolutely necessary that more time should be afforded to prepare the defence. Mr Harry Poland, representing the prosecution, had no objection to this, and since Mr Justice Denman also considered this a reasonable application, he ordered the trial to be postponed until the next sessions.

★

Even as he was languishing in prison awaiting trial for murder, Dr Lamson was fully capable of causing some further mischief. In early 1882, the wealthy gentleman Mr George Mycock had died at Darnall, Sheffield, without leaving a will. His property thus passed to his eldest nephew Edward Mycock, a somewhat dissolute character who had been apprenticed to a chemist in Halifax for a while, before getting a job as a collier. But back in late 1877, the adventurous Edward Mycock had wanted to serve in the Ambulance Corps in the Russo-Turkish War, presumably in some menial capacity. After going abroad, he had completely disappeared: since since none of his relations had ever heard from him again, they had presumed that he had perished in the war. The solicitor handling George Mycock's estate made inquiries with the Red Cross Society, who advised him to seek an interview with George Henry Lamson at the Clerkenwell House of Detention.[7]

On March 7 1882, the solicitor spoke to Dr Lamson, who proved to be most helpful, since he claimed to have met Edward Mycock at Sistova. The bonhomous Doctor willingly signed the following affidavit:

"In the year 1877 I was in the Russian Red Cross service of the sick and wounded. In the month of December, 1877, I was at Sistova on transport service, moving down towards

Plevna to rejoin the column there. Whilst at Sistova my attention was drawn by the officials at the Chancellerie to a person they had informed me was an Englishman who had been captured by the Russians, and who was suffering from illness, and they informed me, that his name was, as they pronounced it, 'Meecocque.' I accordingly visited the said man four or five times in my medical capacity, and found him very seriously ill of either typhus fever or dysentery, – I cannot at this distance of time recollect which. I spoke to him first in English and put some questions to him, and his replies were in English, and were chiefly about his illness and the circumstances under which he had been made a prisoner. I did not have any prolonged conversations with him, as from my medical knowledge of his condition, I could see that the man was dying. He asked me if he was ill, and I remember saying 'Yes, very ill indeed.' I then asked him if I could write to any of his friends for him, and he replied 'Not now,' or 'Not at present.' He mentioned to me that he came from England, and I told him that my friends lived in the Isle of Wight, and asked him if he knew anything about that part of the country. He replied that he did not, and said that he came from further north; but he was in such a state that I prevented his talking much. After I had seen him I moved on by stages to Plevna, but in the course of a week or a fortnight I returned to Sistova, and I inquired at the said Chancellerie, which had the control over the sick and wounded, for the said person, and was told by the officials there that he had died. The staff at the Chancellerie was the same as when I first received information as to the said person being ill. From my medical knowledge I have no doubt that the said person did die, as I considered his recovery perfectly hopeless from the date when I first saw him. But I cannot fix the date of his death any nearer than the month of December, 1877, when I have no doubt it occurred. I have seen the photo annexed, and recognise it as being the photo of the Englishman, whose name I was informed was 'Meecocque,' or 'Mycock,' and whom I have no doubt died as aforesaid."[8]

The Probate and Divorce Division of the High Court of Justice was not a body that believed in rash and hasty action, but on February 20 1883, the Mycock probate case was heard before Sir James Hannen. When Dr Lamson's affidavit was read aloud in court, it appears as if the Doctor's voice from beyond the grave made a very favourable impression in court. The verdict was that since Edward Mycock would be presumed to have died in late 1877, all the property of George Mycock would go to his younger nephew and namesake, who had lived with and worked for his uncle for many years. But the very next day, there was a knock at the door at the solicitor's office: it was Edward Mycock, who had read the newspaper, and decided to make himself known! He explained that he could well remember being attended by Dr Lamson at the Sistova Hospital, where he had been an inpatient with a bullet in the head, among other severe injuries. In the end, he pulled through, and was able to return to Britain in a most emaciated condition. He had not wanted to return to his job as a collier, but had tramped aimlessly around the country; nor had he made any exertions to contact his relations, with whom he was on indifferent terms. He had been foreman at some works in Belmont, Worcestershire, for a while, but lost his situation after going on a drinking spree, and settled down to an idle existence in Malvern. Once, he had called on Dr Lamson, who must have known that Mycock was alive and well when he wrote his affidavit. Thus, the outcome of the case was that the overjoyed Edward Mycock inherited property at Darnall bringing in a rental of several hundred pounds a year: he laughed all the way to the bank, the honest and hard-working nephew wept all the way to the poorhouse, and hollow laughter emanated from Dr Lamson's unmarked grave at Wandsworth Prison.[9]

6. *A postcard showing the gates to Wandsworth Prison.*

*

All of February, the gloomy Doctor sat rattling the bars of his cell in Wandsworth Prison. He was regularly visited by his grieving father, of whose advise he had been deprived when he had needed it the most, and by his loyal wife, whom he had treated so cruelly in his days of decline. In spite of the amount of evidence against her husband, Mrs Lamson was certain that he was innocent, but it remains unknown what degree of solace her selfish husband derived from her childish belief in his inculpability. By this stage, he must have been bitterly regretting turning himself in at Scotland Yard, instead of boarding a fast train out of Paris to make a final gamble with life. Now, his situation resembled that of the heroine in a contemporary popular novel, a bearded damsel in distress, destined to sit impassively at the bar of the Old Bailey, as the prosecuting counsel did their best to ruin him and lead him to the gallows, and the valiant Montagu Williams doing his best for the defence, like a knight fighting Death with a rapier.

But would there be a happy ending in this courtroom drama, like in the sensation novels of Wilkie Collins and Sheridan Le Fanu, or would the knight-errant be defeated, and the heroine left to a dreadful fate? As the Wandsworth prison clock ticked out the remaining hours, minutes and seconds of Dr Lamson's life – 'Tock tick, tock tick, tock tick' – there was an ominous echo of 'Will Death come quick, come quick, come quick? Come quick, come quick, come quick, come quick!'

VIII.

THE TRIAL OF GEORGE HENRY LAMSON

The trial of George Henry Lamson opened at the Central Criminal Court at the Old Bailey on March 8 1882, before Sir Henry Hawkins.[1] The prosecution was led by Sir Farrer Herschell, the Solicitor-General, assisted by Harry Poland and E. Gladstone; the defence was led by Montagu Williams, assisted by Charles Mathews and W.S. Robson, and instructed by the solicitor Arthur Walter Mills. It was called out: The jurors of our Lady, the Queen, upon their oath present, that George Henry Lamson, on the third day of December, in the year of our Lord, one thousand eight hundred and eighty one, feloniously, wilfully, and of his malice aforethought, did kill and murder one Percy Malcolm John, against the peace of our Lady, the Queen, her Crown and dignity. When called upon, Dr Lamson pleaded not guilty.

After the jury had been duly empanelled and sworn, the Solicitor-General opened the case for the crown. The prisoner at the bar stood charged with the gravest offence known to the law, a crime of wilful murder of the most painful character, since the victim had been his own brother-in-law. After reviewing the case against Dr Lamson, he ended his opening speech in ringing tones, exclaiming "Those, then, are the facts which you will have to consider, and you will have to decide to what they point.

1. The exterior of the Old Bailey, a postcard from the series 'Glimpses of Old Newgate'.

2. The Old Court at the Old Bailey.

Left: 3. Sir Henry Hawkins, the judge presiding at the trial of Dr Lamson, from his Reminiscences; *Right: 4. Sir Henry Hawkins and his dog 'Jack', from his* Reminiscences.

5. *Sir Farrer Herschell, the Solicitor-General who prosecuted Dr Lamson, from the* Illustrated London News.

You have the death of this lad occurring after an illness of two or three hours' duration, and after sufferings of the most severe and terrible character. You have not only the causes to account for the death, but you have the symptoms of death from vegetable poison; you have the presence in the body of the deceased – as I think I shall satisfy you beyond the shadow of a doubt – of that most deadly poison aconitine; you have such a poison purchased by the prisoner

Left: 6. Mr Harry Poland, who assisted in the prosecution, from H.L. Adam, The Trial of George Henry Lamson; *Right: 7. A portrait of Montagu Williams, from H.L. Adam,* The Trial of George Henry Lamson.

shortly before; you have the prisoner's own hand administering the last thing he was ever known to have swallowed; you have the prisoner in desperate straits and need of money; you see him in a position to gain a considerable acquisition of fortune by the death of the deceased. Having all these facts, it will be for you to say whether the prisoner is not, however painful it may be to you, guilty of the terrible crime of which he stands charged."

The first witness was William Henry Bedbrook, who described Percy Malcolm John's life at Blenheim House School, saying that although the lad had usually been cheerful, he had at times been despondent. Asked by Sir Henry Hawkins, he added that Percy had been particularly fond of games, although sad not to be able to join the other boys when they were enjoying one. Percy had been his usual self until Dr Lamson had come to call on the evening of December 3. The Doctor had produced a half-empty box of capsules, filled one with sugar, and given it to Percy, who had obediently swallowed it. After a meal of sherry and Dundee cake, the Doctor had made a swift getaway to the railway station. In his agony, Percy had said "I feel as I felt after my brother-in-law had given me a quinine pill at Shanklin." Cross-examined by Montagu Williams, Bedbrook said that when doctors prescribed medicine for his pupils, it was taken care of by the matron and administered either by her or by himself. He was not aware that Percy had planned to spend Christmas with Dr Lamson and his wife, but Williams showed him a postcard written earlier on the day of Percy's death, and addressed to Mrs Lamson, at the Tangmere Hotel near Chichester, stating that the school would break up on December 20 and that he would write again and tell her on which train he was coming. Dr Lamson had once sent Percy a quantity of quinine powders and pills from America, which had been kept in a box. After Percy had swallowed the capsule he had been given by the Doctor, Lamson had cut the cake, and all three had eaten of it. The pupils Walter Edward Banbury and Joseph Bell also gave evidence; the former said that he had once accompanied his friend Percy on a visit to Dr Lamson's house in Bournemouth, and that he had taken one of

8. *Mr Charles Mathews, who assisted in the defence, from H.L. Adam,* The Trial of George Henry Lamson.

the quinine powders from Percy's box without experiencing any ill-effects. This ended the proceedings of the first day of the trial, and the court adjourned at 4.15.

★

The first prosecution witness on the second day of the trial was the matron at Blenheim House School, Mrs Mary Ann Bowles. Before tea on December 3 1881, charades had been played by the boys, Percy included. The crippled lad had been in good health and spirits throughout the day. After Dr Lamson had come calling, Mary Ann Bowles had been asked to bring a sugar-basin. Half an hour later, she had heard that Percy had been taken unwell, and she sat by his sick-bed until the end: "He remained in violent pain until he died; there was no cessation of the pain. He seemed to grow a great deal worse, and had to be held down to his bed." Mrs Bowles was cross-examined by Montagu Williams, who exposed several mistakes and contradictions compared with her testimony at the inquest, although the main body of her evidence remained unscathed. She had once seen Percy make some kind of gas using chemicals, but denied that he had access to any depository of dangerous poisons. Mr Bedbrook, recalled, said that some acids and metal specimens had been kept in a cupboard for the use of the science master Mr Eastwick, but Percy had never used them, nor would he have been able to reach the shelf where they were kept without help.

The classics master Alexander Watt and the assistant master Alfred Godward, who had both seen Percy Malcolm John earlier on December 3, had thought him in his usual health. Godward had also seen Percy after he had been taken ill, retching and vomiting in agony on his bed. The invalid had said that his skin felt all drawn up, and that his mouth was very painful. Importantly, Godward had also heard him say that his brother-in-law had given him a pill, which for some reason he described as a quinine pill when it was in fact a capsule. In the presence of Mrs Bowles, Percy had clearly said "I have taken a quinine pill which my brother-in-law gave me", adding "I took one before at Shanklin, and was nearly as bad then." When Montagu Williams expressed his astonishment at this evidence, and asked why on earth Godward had not appeared at the inquest, the schoolmaster just replied that he had been present, but not examined.

The oddly monickered Dr Other Windsor Berry was the next prosecution witness. As the practitioner looking after the health of the pupils at Blenheim House School, he had known Percy Malcolm John for a year and a half, and once prescribed ointment for some mild skin eruption. He described coming to the school as a guest to an evening party on December 3; when unexpectedly called to Percy's sick-bed, he had found him in a wretched state, retching and vomiting. Dr Berry must have heard some other person (Godward?) mention a quinine pill, since he had said "Did your brother-in-law ever give you a quinine pill before?" "Yes, at Shanklin", the invalid replied. Dr Berry then asked "Did it make you ill like this before?", and the answer was "Yes, but not so bad." To the question "Did your brother-in-law know that it had made you ill like this?", he merely got the answer "I cannot say."

Dr Berry was of course aware that no ordinary quinine pill could have produced symptoms like those suffered by poor Percy. He described his futile efforts to alleviate the torments experienced by the luckless invalid, and the lad's eventual death. He then repeated his declaration that the symptoms suffered by the patient, and the autopsy findings detailed previously, indicated that Percy had died from the administration of an irritant vegetable poison. Dr Berry had been in general practice for 17 years, but he was no close student of toxicology in general, and the workings of vegetable alkaloid poisons in particular. He freely admitted, when examined by Harry Poland, that although various aconitine preparations were used as medicines or ointments, he had never made use of any of them, and that although he believed that aconitine was a very powerful poison, he had never encountered a case of poisoning with this substance before. This line of questioning from the prosecution clearly indicated that they were aware of Dr Berry's various limitations, and that they feared that the clever Montagu Williams would bully the doctor in his cross-examination, exposing his lack of specialist knowledge and defective knowledge about the action of obscure poisons.

And indeed, Montagu Williams had spent much time studying the relevant medical literature, assisted by the celebrated analyst Dr Tidy. This must have been a most tiresome undertaking for a man entirely lacking a medical education: Montagu Williams was an Old Etonian who had started life as a military officer, and then amused himself as a stage actor for a while in Bohemian London, before reading for the Bar and turning to law with considerable success. With a barrage of very unpleasant questions, the peppery 'Monty' Williams soon had Dr Berry literally 'on the ropes': "I think before the magistrate you said that you had not seen a case of poisoning by vegetable alkaloid?" – "Yes"; "And you have no experience of aconitine?" – "No"; "Do you know that aconitine appears in the British Pharmacopœia?" – "No"; "Are you acquainted with a book called 'Fleming on Aconitine'?" – "No". Questioned about the treatment he had administered to the dying boy, Dr Berry explained that his object of injecting morphia had been to allay the pain and nervous irritation; the purpose of making Percy drink white of egg in water had been to alleviate the irritation of the stomach. Montagu William tried to get Dr Berry to admit that Percy's spinal contracture had displaced the lungs or the heart in a sinister manner, thus causing his death, but the doctor resolutely replied that in that case, he would have noticed it at autopsy: in his opinion, the patient's back disease had had nothing to do with his demise.

The next prosecution witness was Dr Edward Stephen Little, of Merton Road in Wimbledon. Examined by Harry Poland, Dr

9. The trial of Dr Lamson at the Old Bailey, from Graphic, *March 18 1882.*

Little described how he and his colleague Dr Berry had attended Percy, adding that they had agreed that the cause of death was the effects of an irritant poison. Cross-examined by Montagu Williams, Dr Little had to admit that he had no experience whatsoever with cases of death by vegetable poisons, however. He could not explain why the stomach pump had never been applied. The autopsy had shown that Percy's curvature of the spine had caused displacement of neither the stomach, nor the lungs or the heart. After a number of policemen had given evidence about the disposal of Percy's pill-box and the quinine powders he had been given by Dr Lamson, the court adjourned at 4.15.

*

After various other police and forensic witnesses had given evidence about the dealing with various items confiscated from Percy's room, and the disposal of the remains from the autopsy for analysis, Dr Thomas Bond was sworn on the morning of the third day. As a lecturer in forensic medicine at Westminster Hospital, he had taken care of various items from Blenheim House School, including the half-eaten Dundee cake, two bags of sweets and some sugar, as well as a pill box and a bottle full of Percy's vomit. He had much experience making post-mortem examinations, and his examination of Percy's body had not indicated that death was due to natural causes; this was in his opinion a case of poisoning with a vegetable alkaloid. Aconitine was a powerful vegetable alkaloid poison, and a lethal dose could have been contained in one of the capsules handled by Dr Lamson.

Cross-examined by the peppery Montagu Williams, Dr Bond had to admit that he had never before seen a case of aconitine poisoning, and that according to the medical literature, this poison was a rarely used one. Montagu Williams tried to lure Dr Bond into expressing an opinion how long it would take from ingestion of aconitine until symptoms of poisoning became apparent, but the doctor, an experienced expert witness, quite correctly replied that this would depend on the nature of the capsule it was administered in, and whether the stomach was full or empty. After the gelatine capsule had been dissolved by the digestive juices, the poison would be absorbed, causing some degree of local intestinal irritation, before being passed into the blood and distributed to the remainder of the body. Traces of a vegetable alkaloid poison would be found in the liver, kidneys and urine.

The next prosecution witness was the shop assistant William Ralph Dodd, from Messrs Allen & Hanbury's chemist business in Plough Court, Lombard Street. He could remember Dr Lamson coming into the shop on November 24 1881 and purchasing two grains of aconitine. Dodd had checked Lamson's name and Bournemouth address in the Medical Directory and found it to be correct, before weighing up the aconitine together with his colleague Charles Betts and selling it to the Doctor for two shillings and sixpence. Cross-examined by Montagu Williams, Dodd said his memory had always been very good. There was a book in the shop into which all purchases of poison must be entered, although not purchases by medical men, so that apart from the testimony of Dodd and Betts, there was no rock solid evidence the Doctor had really made the purchase. Sir Henry Hawkins rightly found it an extraordinary state of affairs that any person with access to the Medical Directory could come walking into a chemist's shop, introduce himself as a doctor, and purchase a quantity of a very dangerous poison.

John Edward Stirling, assistant in the shop of Messrs Bell & Co., chemists of No. 225 Oxford Street, next gave evidence. On November 11, Dr Lamson had come into the shop, introduced himself as a doctor in practice in Bournemouth, and presented a prescription for a solution of morphine and atropine, and five grains of pure digitaline, for his own use. The morphine was duly prepared, but Stirling said that since the shop's stock of digitaline, the active principle of foxglove and a potent poison in the wrong hands, had become badly discoloured, he could not sell any. Some days later, after November 20, Dr Lamson came calling again, with his usual request for a solution of morphine and atropine, for his own use. As the solution was made up, he also asked for one grain of aconitine, for internal use. But since Stirling knew that this was a very potent poison, he refused to provide it, recommending that Lamson should call where he was better known. The Doctor angrily tore up the prescription.

The next witness was David Wavell Littlefield, a chemist at Ventnor. He could remember Dr Lamson coming into his shop on October 13 1880 to purchase some arrowroot, a box of wafer papers and twelve quinine powders. Since the handwriting on the paper enclosed with the quinine powders matched that of Littlefield's assistant, the mystery of the quinine powders found among Percy Malcolm John's effects was a mystery no more.

10. The High Street, Ventnor, where Dr Lamson bought poison at the shop of Charles Albert Smith at No. 76; note the sign saying 'Chemist' to the right of the postcard.

Charles Albert Smith, a chemist at No. 76 High Street, Ventnor, was the next prosecution witness sworn. He knew Dr Lamson, who had been living with his father at 'Mount Vernon', and testified that on August 28 1881, the Doctor had come calling to purchase a stick of Pear's shaving soap, a bottle of Eau de Cologne, three grains of sulphate of atropine, and one grain of aconitine. Knowing that Lamson's family was a respectable one, Smith willingly provided all these items; the purchase was once more not entered into the 'poisons' book since the purchaser was a medical man. Mrs Sophia Jolliffe then introduced herself as the wife of George Jolliffe, of Clarence Villa, Shanklin. William Greenhill Chapman and his wife Margaret Eliza had taken rooms at their lodging-house, bringing with them Percy Malcolm John. Dr Lamson had tea with them on August 28 (or 29), before leaving abruptly. Then Percy got very ill, lying in bed in his ground-floor bedroom and complaining that he felt paralysed all over. Mrs Jolliffe had not stayed with him but advised him to ring the bell if he wanted assistance. He did not ring until 6 am, when he complained that he felt very poorly. His chamber-pot was well filled with excrements, but nevertheless, the invalid went to the closet and remained there for a very long time. Percy then ate his breakfast and gradually recovered.

There was of course a damning temporal connection between Dr Lamson purchasing aconitine in Ventnor and Percy suddenly falling ill after a meal together in Shanklin the very same day, or possibly the day after. Nor is it unreasonable to link this episode to Percy's outcry, on the evening he had died, that his brother-in-law had once given him a quinine pill in Shanklin which had made him very ill. When Montagu Williams asked how Percy had been able to reach the first-floor closet without assistance, Mrs Jolliffe said that he was adept at crawling on his hands and knees, being able to negotiate the stairs, to raise himself from the closet, and to dress himself. She described how she had entered Percy's bedroom when he had rung for assistance early in the morning, to open the window and empty the full chamber-pot.

*

The first prosecution witness on the fourth day of the trial was Dr Thomas Stevenson, lecturer on medical jurisprudence and chemistry at Guy's Hospital. For a period of ten years, he had been employed to make analysis in cases of suspected poisoning. Through the medium of Dr Bond, he had received a number of bottles, containing Percy's liver, spleen and kidneys, intestines, stomach contents, urine and vomit, as well as specimens of the food eaten at table just before Percy had fallen ill, and the contents of the boy's pillbox. Through a modification of Stass's process, he had obtained alkaloidal extracts from the urine, vomit and various body parts. When he applied some of this extract to his tongue, there was a peculiar burning sensation, extending

11. Vignettes from the trial of Dr Lamson, also showing some of the peripheral players in the case: Mr Bedbrook, Mrs Bowles the school matron, the classics master Alexander Watt and Dr Berry, from the Illustrated London News, *March 18 1882.*

down towards the stomach, identical to the sensation produced by aconitine. When some of the extract was injected into the back of a mouse, the creature showed severe symptoms of poisoning after a few minutes and died in thirty minutes, in a similar manner to a mouse injected with aconitine purchased from Allen & Hanbury's chemist's shop. The cake, sherry and sweetmeats contained no poison. The capsules used by the Doctor were made of plain gelatine. It also turned out that some of the quinine powders in Percy's pillbox had been tampered with through the addition of aconitine, as judged by the taste and the lethal effect when it was injected into the back of a mouse. The foolhardy Percy had been playing Russian roulette when taking quinine from this lethal pillbox, as had the pupil Banbury, who had also taken some 'medicine' from Percy's supply.

Questioned by Sir Farrer Herschell, Thomas Stevenson confirmed that one of Dr Lamson's capsules could have contained a lethal dose of aconitine. There was not the slightest doubt that aconitine had been found in the vomit, urine and various body parts. When asked by Montagu Williams whether he had ever seen a case of aconitine poisoning before, Stevenson replied that there had not been such a case in Britain, as far as he was aware, although he knew of a foreign instance of this poison being used. The persistent 'Monty' Williams questioned Dr Stevenson at length about the therapeutic use of aconitine in various diseases, in Britain and abroad, but the knowledgeable doctor withstood this examination unscathed. He was certain the taste he had experienced from the extracts was that of aconitine. He had many times made extracts from the urine and tissues of putrefying corpses without experiencing any similar taste. The mice used in the experiments were tame albino mice that did not object to being handled.

The next prosecution witness was Dr Auguste Dupré PhD, a lecturer on chemistry and toxicology at Westminster Hospital. A native of Germany and a graduate of the University of Heidelberg, he had resided in London for more than 20 years and carried out chemical analysis work for the Home Department. He had helped Dr Stevenson with the analysis of the urine and vomit, and the various organs preserved after the autopsy, and agreed with his superior about the taste of aconitine from the extracts, and the results of the mouse experiments. The next witnesses were Samuel Philip Eastwick and Lawrence John Whalley, who had taught chemistry and physics at Blenheim House School. They agreed that although various acids and salts had been stored in a cupboard at the school, no dangerous poisons had been kept on the premises. John Humphrey Richardson, the assistant of Dr Berry, testified that he had once treated Percy for a skin eruption on the face, with a solution of arsenic, potash and saline. David Ormond, a trustee under the will of the late Mrs John, described her testamentary arrangements, leaving Percy £1991 5s. 11d. in India Four per Cents and £1078 18s. 7d. in Consols, a sum that would be divided between his two surviving sisters if he would die while still a ward in Chancery. The aforementioned William Greenhill Chapman remembered how Percy had been taken ill while visiting him in Shanklin in August 1881. He agreed with Mrs Jolliffe that in spite of his crippled state, Percy could crawl about with alacrity, travelling up and down stairs propelling himself with his arms.

*

On the fifth day of the trial, Mr William Stevenson, editor of the *Bournemouth Observer*, described how Dr Lamson had borrowed more than £100 from him, before absconding to America. Edward Wyse Rebbeck, the agent for the owner of 'Hursley', described how he had sent in the bailiffs when the Doctor failed to pay the rent. The upholsterer James Croome had only been able to recover £14 6s. 7d. of the £63 4s. 3d. that Dr Lamson owed to him for goods supplied. The unfortunate Thomas Cullan, a

Fellow of the Institute of Chartered Accountants, who was owed £200 by the deceitful Doctor, never saw his money again. Price Owen described how Dr Lamson had cheated him out of £20 with a dishonoured cheque. The somewhat mysterious medical student John Law Tulloch described his expedition to Wimbledon with Dr Lamson on December 2, with liberal drinks breaks on the way at various pubs. He felt certain that the Doctor had told him that he had just been to see his brother-in-law, whose health was very much worse, so that he would not live much longer. Tulloch had met Dr Lamson from time to time for several years, although there had recently been an estrangement between them, due to the dishonoured cheque for £12 10s. that Tulloch had cashed for his friend. In the past, he had borrowed money from Dr Lamson from time to time, but always repaid it. Tulloch's brother William had fonder memories of Dr Lamson, who had lent him money more than once; when the Doctor, by now impecunious himself, had gone to pawn his case of surgical instruments and a gold hunting watch in late November 1881, it was to get some money for William Tulloch, who was in very dire straits indeed. The hotel keeper James Creighton Nelson then testified as to his dealings with Dr Lamson, and the Doctor's two letters to him, about lending him £5 and about purchasing some Dundee cake on credit, were read aloud in court, with the comment that neither request was complied with. It was Lamson who had the last laugh, however, successfully absconding from the hotel without paying his bill. William Greenhill Chapman read the letter he had received from Dr Lamson in Paris, and Inspector Butcher described how the Doctor had given himself up at Scotland Yard. The final prosecution witness was George Lamb, a porter at the Wimbledon railway station, who described meeting Dr Lamson there, and receiving an envelope with some money inside as a last-minute 'tip' for poor Percy.

Realizing the key importance of the medical evidence in the Lamson case, Montagu Williams had hoped to employ a medical expert of his own to assess the analysis of Percy's remains, but the Secretary of State decided not to allow the presence of another medical man, since this was contrary to all practice. In his memoirs, 'Monty' Williams does not mention whether he had considered finding medical witnesses to stand up and contradict Dr Bond and Dr Stevenson, but failed in the attempt. The fact remains that Williams did not have any witnesses to call for the defence, although he made use of all his eloquence in a long speech, of which he was so proud that he included it as an appendix to his memoirs. He placed before the jury two propositions. Firstly, had Percy Malcolm John died from the ingestion of aconitine, beyond any reasonable doubt? If there was reasonable doubt on this point, the prisoner at the bar was entitled to be acquitted. Secondly, if the jury was of the opinion beyond all reasonable doubt that Percy had died from aconitine poisoning, the question remained whether the poison had been wilfully administered by the prisoner.

The medical evidence in the Lamson case was most vague and unreliable, Montagu Williams asserted: "Who knows anything about aconitine? And echo answers 'Who?'" When Dr Berry and Dr Little had attended Percy, they had failed to provide the boy with remedies and not used the stomach pump, but still they asserted, with the benefit of hindsight, that they had suspected that he had been suffering from the effects of a vegetable irritant poison. The opinion of Dr Bond had been misled by the that of Dr Berry and Dr Little, namely that this was a case of poisoning. Unlike the other three doctors, Dr Stevenson actually had good knowledge of aconitine, although even he had admitted never seeing a case of poisoning with this substance. It should be noted, however, that Stevenson had determined the presence of aconitine in the various extracts by taste only, surely a most fallible test that could not be relied upon to swear away a man's life. Little tame mice were highly timorous creatures, Montagu Williams asserted: they could die just from the shock of being picked up, or from the prick of a needle. Thus the animal experiments conducted by Dr Stevenson were equally fallible: the feeble mice had just died at random when their asthenic constitutions had been challenged during the experiments, meaning that under no circumstances, the jury could agree that Percy Malcolm John had been poisoned with aconitine.

"Now comes the question", Montagu Williams continued, "should you be of the opinion that this was a case of aconitine poisoning, who administered it?" Dr Lamson had always been very fond of his young brother-in-law, he asserted: the bonhomous Doctor had often invited him to his house or visited him at Blenheim House School. It was a monstrous thought that Dr Lamson would murder the trusting young lad for the paltry sum of £1 500 to be handed over to his wife. It was true that at the time of the death of Percy Malcolm John, the Doctor was facing great poverty, but poverty was not a crime: "To be unfortunately poor is one thing, but to commit an infamous and monstrous crime for the sake of obtaining money is another thing." There was no doubt, Montagu Williams asserted, that in early December 1881, Percy Malcolm John's general health left much to be desired: his severe curvature of the spine may well have contributed to his death. No poison had been found in the food brought to the school by Dr Lamson, including the Dundee cake; no person had seen him load the capsule with poison; it was, furthermore, just a mere theory that he had put sugar in the capsule for the purpose of disguising the poison. Moreover, evidence that some of the prosecution witnesses had actively sought to conceal spoke in favour that, in spite of his crippled state, Percy was able to crawl from one room to another, and even to negotiate a flight of stairs. Would it not have been possible that with his usual fondness for taking medicine, Percy had crawled over to some cupboard and helped himself to some noxious substance kept in there? As for the letter sent to Percy by Dr Lamson from the Wimbledon railway station, containing a tip of four shillings and sixpence, was this not a sign of innocence and brotherly love rather than some diabolical scheme to disguise the Doctor's guilt?

★

On the sixth and final day of the trial, Montagu Williams continued his lengthy speech for the defence. He bitterly complained that the Home Secretary had not allowed an independent analyst to be present to represent the prisoner. The two witnesses Dodd and Betts, from Allen & Hanbury's chemist's shop, had dithered whether it had been aconitine or atropine that Dr Lamson had purchased, before finding an entry for 2s 6d for an item sold to a medical man; since aconitine was 1s 3d per grain this proved, to their satisfaction, that the Doctor had purchased two grains of aconitine. But Montagu Williams knew that Dr Lamson always took atropine with his morphine, and he found an entry in the sales ledger for 8d worth of chemicals sold to a medical man – could this be Dr Lamson and his atropine? As for Mr Stirling, of Messrs Bell's of Oxford Street, he had only testified that Dr Lamson had wanted to buy a grain of aconitine, clearly to make an ointment to treat his own neuralgia and rheumatism, conditions to which he was a martyr according to his friend William Tulloch.

As for Mr Littlefield, the Shanklin chemist who had sold quinine powders to Dr Lamson, the prosecution had suggested that these were the powders turning up in Percy's pill-box. Moreover, Mr Bedbrook had testified that Dr Lamson had sent Percy some pills from America, one of which had made him ill; these pills had been destroyed according to Mr Bedbrook. Montagu Williams expressed astonishment as to the well-filled state of Percy's pill-box, with a multitude of capsules and loose pills lying about. Of the quinine powders analysed by Dr Stevenson, one had been claimed to contain aconitine, but still he had not tested them all. Then we had Albert Smith, the Shanklin chemist who had sold Dr Lamson three grains of atropine and one grain of aconitine on August 28 1880. Percy Malcolm John had come to Shanklin on August 27 and had fallen ill the following day, but this was just an upset digestion and not a case of poisoning at all, Montagu Williams claimed. As for the two Tulluchs, Williams treaded lightly when it came to Brother William, who had after all testified that Dr Lamson suffered from neuralgia and rheumatism. As for the hard-drinking John Law Tulloch, the experienced barrister reminded the jury that he had asked William Tulloch "Is your brother, late in the afternoon, sometimes the worse for liquor?", although this question had been disallowed after Sir Farrer Herschell had objected to it.

Montagu Williams pointed out that although Dr Lamson had taken the train to Paris, he had made no attempt to escape from justice, but come to Scotland Yard to be taken before the magistrate, like an innocent man would. As for the motive for the murder, supposed to be to obtain £1 500, was this not fallacious reasoning, since no money would have been paid over if there was suspicion of foul play. Williams ended his speech in ringing tones: "Gentlemen, I now come to what is to me the most painful part of my duty. I have told you that you have the life of a fellow-creature in your hands. In reality you have a trinity of lives in your hands. You have three people to consider. This man has a wife. Who stood by him in the hour of poverty? That wife. Did you notice her on the first day? A thin, spare figure came up to the dock and took him by the hand, saying by her presence, 'Though all men be against you, though all the world be against you, in my heart there is room for you still.' Gentlemen, they say that women are inferior creatures, but in the hour of retribution it may be said of women –

When pain and anguish wring the brow,
A ministering angel thou.

She had sworn at the altar to love, honour and obey him. It is well that the compilers of the solemn service put 'love' first, for where there is woman's love the others follow, as a matter of course; and up to this moment she has stood, so to speak, by his side. Gentlemen, if the prisoner be convicted, and his life be sacrificed, what a legacy is there for her! What a reward for all her true nobility, and for all that is softest and best in life – a widowed home, a cursed life, and a poor little child never to be taught to lisp its father's name, its inheritance the inheritance of Cain!"

"I make these observations, gentlemen, not with any desire to make you deviate by one hair's breadth from the path of duty that you are bound to tread; but I do make them to beg, to entreat, to beseech you, with these last tones of my voice, not to found your

Lowers her pale face and weeps.'

12. *Mrs Lamson weeps as Montagu Williams makes a speech in court, from* Famous Crimes Past & Present.

verdict upon speculative theories and visionary ideas; but to test, and try, and weigh – and accurately weigh – every particle of the evidence – real, solid, cogent evidence – before you come to a verdict antagonistic to this man. Into your hands I commend a brother's life, for, no matter what our nationality or creed may be, by the common tie of human nature all men are brothers. I can only beg you, lastly, to extend towards him – your brother – that upon which, in my humble judgment, all true religion is founded; do unto him, your brother, as you would if you were placed in such dire straits, that your brethren should do unto you, and may the Lord direct you rightly."

★

As Montagu Williams sat down after his long speech, Sir Farrer Herschell stood up. He kept his closing speech for the prosecution short and to the point. The cause of the death of Percy Malcolm John was clearly poisoning, as suspected by the doctors attending him at the time; why would they otherwise have collected his vomit, and taken charge of the wafers and cake? The analysis made by Thomas Stevenson clearly demonstrated that the poison used was aconitine, as judged by the sense of taste and by the mouse experiments. Whatever was thought of the witness Tulloch, his testimony suggested that on December 2, Dr Lamson had gone to Wimbledon with what must be suspected was murderous intent, "but that his heart failed him, and he shrank from doing what he had contemplated and which he succeeded in doing the following evening."

The prosecution had proved that shortly before the murder of Percy Malcolm John, Dr Lamson had purchased aconitine at Allen & Hanbury's pharmacy. And was there not a sinister similarity to his earlier attempt on Percy's life at Shanklin: the purchase of poison, illness of the boy, and speedy escape of the Doctor. The motive was clearly financial gain: Dr Lamson "was in straitened and desperate need of money; he was drawing fictitious cheques, and so pressed for money that he was tempted to bring himself within the power of the criminal law." It was in his favour that he had returned to face justice in London, but he had done so believing that the poison he had administered would not be detected, and that the only thing in his disfavour was his escape to Paris; moreover, he had been without means and without prospects, and unable to make his escape even if he had wanted to.

Sir Farrer ended his final speech with the words: "You have now heard the whole facts of this case. It is not your duty to weigh the consequences of the verdict, or to be influenced by them. You must judge by the facts, stifling emotion, and shutting your eyes to the consequences. If, so judging the case, clouds of doubt arise in your minds, then let the prisoner have the benefit; but if you should be of the opinion that the facts have been brought home without doubt, then, by the duty you owe to society, and for the safety of the public, you are bound to give your verdict against him."

After Sir Henry Hawkins had summed the case up in his charge to the jury, the jurymen were out for just half an hour, being asked by the Clerk of Arraigns: "Gentlemen, are you all agreed?" "We are." replied the Foreman.

"Do you find the prisoner, George Henry Lamson, guilty or not guilty?"

"Guilty."

"Prisoner at the bar, have you anything to say why the Court should not give you judgment according to law?"

"Merely to protest my innocence before God." replied the Doctor in a firm voice.

Mr Wilson, the Chief Usher, demanded silence for Mr Justice Hawkins to pass sentence.

"George Henry Lamson, the jury having convicted you of the crime of wilful murder, the law commands me to pass upon you the sentence of death. It would serve no good end were I to recapitulate the harrowing details of your cruel, base, and treacherous crime; nor it is part of my office to admonish you how to meet the dread doom that awaits you. Suffice it to say that I entreat you to prepare to meet Almighty God, and may He pardon you your great sin. The sentence of the Court upon you is that you be taken from hence to the place from whence you came, thence to a lawful place of execution, and that there you be hanged by your neck until you be dead, and, when you are dead, your body buried within the precincts of that prison wherein you were last confined after the passing of this judgment upon you. And may the Lord have mercy upon your soul."

As the wretched Doctor was removed, Mr Justice Hawkins thanked the jury for their great attention to duty, promising them that their suggestion that the law as to the sale of poisons required amendment would be forwarded to the Home Secretary.

IX.

RESPITE AND AFFIDAVITS

The newspaper press commented approvingly on the verdict in the Wimbledon poisoning case, agreeing with the jury that Dr Lamson was the guilty man. A *Daily News* editorial summed it up: "The proof of Lamson's guilt was really overwhelming, and the prosecution might easily have dispensed with the old and questionable privilege which gives counsel for the Crown the right of reply, even when no evidence is called for the prisoner, whenever the proceedings are instituted directly by the Treasury. It is satisfactory to know that one more substance has been withdrawn from the repository of the occult poisoner, and that the attention of the whole medical profession has been forcibly drawn to the strength, the properties, and the tests of aconitine." *Reynolds's Newspaper* thought that "A more diabolical villain than Lamson never stood in the dock at the Old Bailey. He turned his talents, and the education he had acquired, to the worst and vilest account …" A correspondent of the *Daily Telegraph* fully acquiesced in the justice of the verdict that doomed Dr Lamson to an ignominious death, but he had met the Doctor in happier days during the Russo-Turkish war, and could not understand how so amiable, gifted and accomplished a man could possibly have committed a crime that was the negation of his entire past life story.[1] The following day, the High Sheriff of Surrey fixed the day of the execution of George Henry Lamson as Tuesday April 4.

In his column in the *Referee* weekly newspaper, the eloquent poet and playwright George R. Sims gave his views on the Lamson affair: "The Lamson trial seems to have disappointed the people who expected fun out of it. That a large class exist who look upon murder trials as things specially got up for their amusement, no one who reads the 'special intro's' in the dailies can doubt. ... All poisoners are cowardly and detestable wretches, and Lamson seems to have been as cowardly as any of them. Yet there is no doubt that in other places and under other circumstances the man has won hosts of friends by his bravery, his bonhomie, and his self-denying attention to the sick and wounded committed to his care. It seems difficult, his former acquaintances confess, to believe that the knightly Lamson of old days and the cowardly poisoner of the crippled boy can be one and the same person. The people who express the greatest astonishment at the apparent contradiction of character are those who know the least about human nature. Hundreds of men who are the heroes of life's melodrama under one set of circumstances become its villains under another. There are plenty of us who are good and brave and noble simply because the opportunity and the temptation to be otherwise do not occur. Lust and greed are at the bottom of most of our criminal romances. It is extraordinary to what depths of depravity men will descend under the influence of the two great dominating passions. ... Yet with such a life-history as that of Lamson laid bare under the searching eye of Justice, the polished villains of melodrama sink into insignificance."[2]

It did not take long for the Rev. Mr Lamson to activate his 'Plan B' after the guilty verdict on March 14. He joined Mrs Kate Lamson to visit his son at Wandsworth Prison on March 15. They brought with them a letter from Dr Lamson to a London friend of his, praising the efforts of the solicitor Mills and the eloquent Montagu Williams, although the latter should have called a number of witnesses for the defence regarding the Doctor's good character, "traceable through many years down to a day or two previous to my departure to Paris and the poor boy's death."[3] Already on March 17, there was a newspaper report that the Rev. Gentleman was making exertions, among friends both in Britain and the United States, to prove that his son's habit of injecting morphine and atropine had long been affecting his mind, leading to extreme forgetfulness, and the making of reckless and untrue statements. For example, when meeting a clergyman friend in the Isle of Wight after his first visit to America, he explained the reason for his arm being in a sling as a desperate fight against some Italians in Liverpool, whereas the truth was that he had developed abscesses in the arm through his misuse of morphine, and had been lancing them.[4]

1. *The Home Secretary Sir William Harcourt, from Vol. 2 of A.G. Gardiner,* Life of Sir William Harcourt *(London 1923).*

On March 17, Dr Lamson was visited by the solicitor Arthur Walter Mills, who was helping the Rev. Gentleman with tracking down witnesses. The Doctor conducted himself with much composure, spending his time mostly reading and writing. He no longer felt any craving for morphia, his appetite had improved, and he was able to sleep soundly at night. At Clerkenwell he had been nearly starved, but the food at Wandsworth Prison was much better, he said.[5] On Sunday March 19, Dr Lamson attended services at the Prison Chapel at Wandsworth, hearing the Rev.

Mr Gilbert preach about the Prodigal Son. On March 20, when Mrs Lamson again visited her husband in prison, the Rev. Mr Lamson had roughly drafted his memorial to the Home Secretary, and was actively searching for witnesses in Bournemouth and elsewhere, to prove that even if his son had administered poison to his victim, he had been unaccountable for his actions at the time.[6] A news bulletin said that the Doctor was very grateful that his father and friends were doing everything they could to save him from the gallows. He had no confession to make and no fear of death; if his brother-in-law Percy Malcolm John had met death at his hands it must have been by misadventure, for he could not recollect ever having entertained one thought against the boy's life.[7] Mrs Julia Lamson, the convict's mother, had been lying ill in Paris, but she had come to London on March 24, when the Home Secretary granted a permission for Dr Lamson's wife and parents to see him in prison without double rows of iron bars separating them, and only with the chief warder present.[8]

★

The Bournemouth affidavits in favour of Dr Lamson's insanity are a queer lot.[9] There was a story that the Doctor had once, as a Lieutenant in the Bournemouth Artillery Volunteers, been in charge of a guard of honour. He wore a number of medals, which he said he had earned by his valiant efforts on the European battlefields. He pointed out his Iron Cross, saying that when the Emperor William of Germany had seen him actively at work in the field hospital outside Paris, looking after the wounded, he had removed the Iron Cross from his own breast and attached it to Lamson's. On investigation, it turned out that the deceitful Doctor had purchased both his Iron Cross and another medal, said to have emanated from the hand of the Sultan of Turkey, in some shop for military memorabilia.[10] The spinster Ellen Pocock, who lived near Southampton, had known Dr Lamson for 10 years, and stayed in his Rotherfield house from June until September 1878, without making any detrimental observations concerning his mental health. But when she again went to visit the Doctor and his wife in Bournemouth in November 1881, she thought him peculiar in his manner: wandering, nervous and restless. He was under the delusion that he had a friend named Arkwright, from whom he was constantly expecting presents. He ate very little and habitually abstained from joining in the family meals.

The surveyor Arthur Joseph Salter had met Dr Lamson about once a week during his residence in Bournemouth. Since the Doctor's eyes "betrayed a look of wildness" and since his facial expression "was that of a man whose reason was affected", Salter thought him insane. The Bournemouth artist William Joseph Warren, who had known Dr Lamson in 1880 and 1881, also thought him of unsound mind: "His eyes had a fitful and nervous look as if he was in fear of phantoms. He seemed perpetually making an effort to appear sane." Warren had seen the Doctor injecting morphine with a hypodermic syringe, and he thought these excesses responsible for his mental quirks. The gentleman Radclyffe Radclyffe-Hall retold the sorry tale of Dr Lamson's libel on his wife, adding that the Doctor had been in the habit of telling various tall and unlikely stories. Once, he had said that he had travelled from America to Paris in a balloon; another time, that he was an expert diver who could remain under water for 25 minutes.[11] The Bournemouth auctioneer William Arthur Marshall, who had known Dr Lamson since 1879, found him very absent-minded, and subject to the most extraordinary delusions and fears. Two witnesses, Lydia Humphreys who had brought her consumptive sister to Bournemouth, and Arthur John Hawkes whose wife had been ill, signed affidavits as to Dr Lamson's strange behaviour towards his patients. John Webber, keeper of the South Western Hotel in Bournemouth, who had Dr Lamson as a guest on November 28 1881, was very much struck by his extraordinary manner and conversation, thinking that he must have escaped from a lunatic asylum. Three of the doctors consulted by Dr Lamson in Ventnor or London testified as to his extensive morphine abuse.

The Rev. Mr Lamson and the solicitor Mills had also done a good job tracking down his son's former domestics during his declining years in Bournemouth. The nurse Mary Mugford, who had entered the Doctor's service in June 1880, found him very queer indeed, ordering the servants about and then denying that he had done so, and ringing the study and dining room bells at all times. He laboured under various delusions: that he had been attacked by robbers, or seriously stabbed. She testified that he had been insane and not responsible for his actions. The coach builder John Jephta Edmunds, who had been employed by Dr Lamson from 1879 until 1881, found him incapable of talking rationally, with a strange unsettled look on his face; his wife Elizabeth, who also signed an affidavit, agreed that he was of unsound mind. Ellen King, the former cook at 'Hursley' also found her master very queer; the other servants never listened to him, he could not talk rationally, and he once fired a revolver out of the bedroom window for no reason at all. Mary Ann Smith, the former housemaid, found that her master was full of childish fears and fancies; he was unable to talk rationally and practically had no memory at all. He frequently ordered her about and then denied giving her any instructions. Charles Taylor, who had entered the service of Dr Lamson as a coachman in October 1880, said that his master had been paranoid, fearing that unknown men would come to kill him, and insisting that Taylor should carry a revolver to be able to return fire. He often rang the bell to summon Taylor, only to have forgotten the reason when the exasperated coachman appeared. The servants paid little attention to his instructions, since his behaviour was so very queer; Taylor once told his colleagues that Dr Lamson belonged in a lunatic asylum, and that he would be in one before six months had passed.

The Rev. Mr Lamson had also been able to track down a number of dissatisfied patients complaining about his son's odd behaviour when attending them in Bournemouth. The coffee tavern keeper George Lawson, who kept a dispensary in his Bournemouth house, testified that few patients wanted to see Dr Lamson there, due to his odd behaviour, preferring the other doctor on duty. The gardener Charles Davis also thought Dr Lamson quite deranged: after attending Mrs Davis or other family members, he would not leave but stand in the garden like a man stupefied for half an hour, occasionally rubbing his hand against his face. John and Emily Petty, of the Woodman Tavern in Bournemouth, decided to call in another doctor after seeing Lamson's strange behaviour while attending Mrs Petty in confinement. When the clumsy Doctor delivered the child of Elizabeth Ames, he broke its arm and took it to his house for treatment instead of at once setting the fracture. When he attended Julia Lydford in confinement, he sat rubbing his hands without giving the slightest attention to her. When he treated the daughter of Mary Kavanagh, he went away and never came back although the patient was supposed to have been gravely ill. In all, nine dissatisfied patients provided affidavits for the Rev. Mr Lamson, and also the monthly nurse Jane Cuff, who complained of the Doctor's contradictory orders to her.[12]

Since there was much newspaper interest in the struggle to save Dr Lamson from the gallows, the Home Office folder of correspondence from the general public is well filled with letters.[13] Mr G. Latham Browne, of the Temple, wanted to see the medical evidence in the Smethurst and Lamson cases, but this was denied him.[14] From the Royal Albion Hotel, Brighton, Lord Clifton wrote a long letter arguing that Percy had been poisoned by the diseased rabbit and onion stew he had eaten, entirely by mistake. The dotty Peer knew that the doctors were a vindictive lot, who had perjured themselves to get rid of the Transatlantic rival Lamson by whatever means possible. Lord Clifton also wrote to the *Times*, arguing that the medical evidence was inconclusive and that Dr Lamson was innocent.[15] Dr H. Arthur Allbutt wrote a letter to the *Leeds Express* arguing that Lamson might have given Percy aconitine as a medicine, and that in his weakened and susceptible state, Percy had succumbed to it; thus the Doctor's guilt was not proven. He also wrote to the Home Office calling for a reprieve.[16] Dr Paul B. Connolly, of the Army Medical Department at Aldershot, knew Dr Lamson from the Russo-Turkish war of 1877. When they had met in Serbia and Roumania, the Doctor had not been a morphine addict, nor had he had any particular interest in aconitine. From Thurloe Square, Kensington, Dr John James wrote to the Home Office to suggest that Percy Malcolm John had in fact died from the morphine injection administered by Dr Berry. Dr W. Hempson Denham, a Southsea practitioner, argued that Percy had died from unrelated causes, possibly indigestion from eating the Dundee cake; the analysts were all wrong, and Dr Lamson was an innocent man. A certain George Bolton, who called himself 'A Working Man', claimed that he had read every word about the Lamson case; he urged that the Doctor should be executed for committing a very cruel murder. Carlo Mappono, a Rome journalist, who was writing a treatise on the 'Sistems [sic] of Law Punishments in England', wanted to witness the execution of Lamson, but that particular honour was denied him.

★

The original intention was that the memorial to the Home Secretary should be sent in on March 27, but this was rendered impossible by the exertions of the solicitor Mills, who was in Bournemouth searching for further affidavits from people who had known Dr Lamson. Mills found that at one Bournemouth chemist's shop, Dr Lamson had purchased seven ounces of morphia in a month, and that in another, there was an account for morphia amounting to £12.[17] The problem was that the set date for Dr Lamson's execution, April 4, was approaching with rapidity, and that a wealth of American affidavits were still on their way across the Atlantic. On March 27, the Rev. Mr Lamson and Mr Mills convened a meeting for 50 prominent Americans resident in London, at the Exeter Hall; the outcome was that much sympathy was expressed for Dr Lamson's plight, and that a committee of three was appointed to approach the American Minister, the anglophile poet and literary man James Russell Lowell. The Rev. Mr Lamson had made full use of his not inconsiderable transatlantic contacts, and he knew that Lowell already had a petition forwarded through the State Department of Washington, signed by two Episcopalian bishops and many New York clergymen, asking that Lowell should approach the Home Secretary with regard to the insanity of the convict Lamson.[18]

The memorial presented by the Rev. Mr Lamson and the solicitor Mills was finally delivered to the Home Secretary on March 29, when the Doctor had only six more days to live. James Russell Lowell showed himself as a man of action: already on March 28, he wrote a formal letter to the Foreign Secretary, Earl Granville, pointing out that President Chester Arthur had been approached by a committee of bishops and clergymen, asking that the execution of Dr Lamson should be postponed, to enable the American affidavits concerning his insanity to be properly pondered.

2. A postcard showing James Russell Lowell, US Minister in London.

On March 30, US Secretary of State Frederick Theodore Frelinghuysen sent a telegram to Minister Lowell, asking him once more to intervene with Earl Granville, to make sure that Dr Lamson was respited; the US Attorney General had been consulted, and considered that there was a proper case for such interference, awaiting the arrival of the documentary evidence from the United States, tending to demonstrate the prisoner's insanity and the absence of a criminal intent.[19]

After taking a few days to ponder the situation, Home Secretary Sir William Harcourt made his decision on April 1: the execution of the convict Lamson was respited until April 18 for the American evidence to be properly considered, as President Chester Arthur had requested through Minister Lowell. The very same day, Dr Lamson was visited by his father and wife, who gave him the good news and had a long interview with him; the Doctor expressed his gratitude for the favour of the authorities, and was much cheered by the efforts of his father and Mr Mills on his behalf.[20] On April 3, Sir R. Assheton Cross asked a question in Parliament, whether that morning's news story with regard to the convict Lamson was true, and in that case what was the reason for this unexpected respite? Sir William Harcourt replied that through the Foreign Office, he had received a request from the Minister of the United States of America, dated March 31,

3. A postcard showing the US President Chester A. Arthur, who also took an interest in the Lamson case.

saying that it was the personal wish of President Chester Arthur that the execution of Dr Lamson should be suspended until certain evidence collected and transmitted to the Attorney General of the United States had been inspected at the Home Office. There were several precedents of such respites being granted awaiting evidence in difficult cases.[21] When Mr Mills came to see him on April 4, Dr Lamson was cheered with the good news: his spirits were much revived, and he now felt confident that with the help of the American affidavits, he would be saved from the gallows.

There was much uproar in the London newspapers after Dr Lamson had been respited. The *Daily News* and the *Morning Post* both approved of the decision, pointing out that it was a very grave step to order a man's execution when there were documents on their way allegedly proving his insanity at the time of the murder, and that the President of the United States of America was a personage who should be listened to when it came to matters of state. The *Times* chose a middle-of-the-road approach: as foreigners, the only option of Lamson's American friends was to approach their own government, and it was good that the plea of insanity, sprung upon the Home Secretary after four months of silence about the alleged evidence, should be properly investigated. After all, there were rumours, spread by Lamson's friends in London, that the American affidavits would show that the Doctor had the blight of hereditary insanity in his blood, and that he had a mania for giving people aconitine. The *Standard* showed a staunch anti-Lamson attitude, boldly claiming that the Home Secretary had made a decided mistake in giving in to the President's request, since it created a dangerous precedent that undermined one of the central principles of international law, namely that an alien who violates the criminal law of a civilized state is amenable to that law alone. The *Daily Telegraph* agreed, describing the announcement as startling, and pointing out that "According to English law, drunkenness – and the results of taking morphia are similar to any other intoxication

– is no excuse for a crime, unless it has produced mental disease which prevents a person from knowing that his act is wrong."[22] The New York papers generally showed a pro-Lamson attitude, expressing satisfaction that the execution had been respited; after all, many Americans were opponents of capital punishment, at least when it involved one of their own number in a foreign land, and the Rev. Mr Lamson was widely respected in religious circles.

In the 1880s, London had a considerable population of 'funny' weekly newspapers, many of them cheap and down-market imitators of the popular *Punch*. After George Henry Lamson had been found guilty of murder and sentenced to death, the flow of sympathy for the murderer from transatlantic sources was very much disapproved of by these newspapers. Anti-American witticisms abounded, of which the following is a fair example: "Uncle Sam, to whom we owe dynamite, Fenianism, and the use of the revolver, has sent us an imperative message to stay the execution of Lamson until further orders. We are long suffering, we would do much to satisfy Uncle Sam, but we really ought to be allowed to hang Lamson if we please, we must draw the line somewhere."[23] The *Moonshine* weekly paper exclaimed that "Lamson is, as was to be expected, to be petitioned for. Everybody is petitioned for nowadays, and the worse the case the louder the outcry. The ground of the application in this cruellest and most cowardly of recent instances is the inadequacy of the mouse test. All but the petitioners are convinced; what can be simpler, if the poison is not a poison, than to disprove the mouse test by aconitining the petitioners?"[24] When the novelist Charles Reade wrote a letter to argue in favour of the insanity of Dr Lamson, quoting his libel on the wife of the gentleman Radclyffe Radclyffe-Hall as an example of his mind becoming increasingly deranged, the *Sporting Times* was quick to retort that "If Charles Reade's letter to the *Daily Telegraph* of Thursday does not get Lamson off, it will at any rate ensure, should he murder half England, Charles Reade's not being hung. And where did

Charles Reade spring that 'baronet and his wife' from in his letter to the *D.T.* anent Mr Poisoner Lamson? Mr R. Radclyffe Hall is the son of a respected Torquay physician, not the possessor of a 'bloody hand'."[25] *Funny Folks* was inspired by the Lamson affair to 'lapse into poetry':

"Do I recall the Lamson case? Well, rather, I should say,
And how the affidavits kept arriving day by day,
And how at length we were obliged by Presidential power
To go and respite Lamson every quarter of an hour!
We soon became accustomed to restrain our penal zeal,
And we always granted culprits an American appeal.
Our judges sentenced as of yore, while adding with a leer,
That is, of course, if Arthur doesn't choose to interfere."[26]

★

The Rev. Mr Lamson visited his son in Wandsworth Prison on April 6. The very same day, a letter he had written to the *Times* was published: "The general tone of the public Press upon the subject of the respite accorded to my son, Dr Lamson, forces upon me the unwelcome duty of breaking the silence I would gladly preserve could I permit the thought that the family of the condemned are resorting to unrealities or subterfuges to reverse a judgment generally accepted by the public as just." Dr Lamson had been too proud to appeal to his family for money, although he had been aware that he merely had to stretch out his hand for such help, the Rev. Gentleman asserted. When he made that deplorable visit to Wimbledon, he was in fact on his way from a devoted wife to equally solicitous parents, the Rev. Mr Lamson asserted, bending the truth a good deal. Dr Lamson's diseased brain was "wrought upon by ill-health, personal anxieties, professional work, and greatly aggravated by the baneful use of narcotics." Had the defence not made the "grave omission" not to follow the Rev. Mr Lamson's recommendation to 'play the insanity card' and point out the obvious mental derangement of the prisoner at the dock, this would have greatly changed the aspect of the case to the jury. The Britons were a high-minded and gracious people, the Rev. Gentleman continued, and he felt sure they would listen to the exhortations of the family of the convict Lamson, left to languish in Wandsworth Prison awaiting an uncertain fate. "But it is not too much to hope that these explanations not only be received as an avowal on my part of the truthfulness of the plea now urged, and supported by a mass of strong sworn testimony, but that it may gather about my unhappy son those sympathies which are, in the English people, ever at the call of fairness and suffering, to help them to the belief that a young man, ever distinguished for gentleness and generosity, highly educated and religiously trained, ever ready to succour human misery, was as little likely as any man to become what he is now judged to be, without a dethronement of that intelligence which regulates all our natural instincts."[27]

The first batch of the American evidence, dispatched on the *Arizona* on April 5, reached Mr Mills on April 14. It was copied and sent to the Home Office, with a letter asking for a further respite in order that the whole of the testimony already sworn and dispatched may be laid before the Home Secretary. John Dawson Watson, who had been in the billiard room at the Eyre Arms, had seen his friend John Law Tulloch play with Dr Lamson. Since he thought Lamson looked like a man without reason, he had taken Tulloch aside and said:

"John, who is your lunatic friend?"

"He is a very dear and old friend of mine, a very fine surgeon and a clever fellow."

"I am very sorry, but he is mad all the same!"

There was also a letter from Mr William Phillips, secretary of the Municipal Reform League, who had been travelling on a train about two weeks prior to the murder. All of a sudden, Dr Lamson came bounding into the compartment, introduced himself, and did many mad things. He said he had been shot in the head, the lungs and the legs, and that he had just come from the bedside of President Garfield, whom he had been attending. He flourished a large medical instrument, which he said was for cutting off legs, and waved it about in such a dangerous manner that Mr Phillips was quite happy when another person came into the compartment. According to a newspaper report, Dr Lamson's health was quite good at the present time, after he had been weaned off the morphine; his appetite was in no way impaired, he slept well, and his spirits were at times almost buoyant. He seemed to have a fixed idea that after all his father's work to

4. *Dr Lamson, in prison attire, is informed about his respite, from the* Illustrated Police News, *April 15 1882.*

rescue him from the scaffold, the capital sentence would not be carried out. He had written what was purported to be a diary of his movements just before his visit to Wimbledon, but it turned out to be entirely unreliable, since many of its statements had been proven wrong.[28]

On April 16, Sir William Harcourt wrote a letter to the Sheriff of Surrey that George Henry Lamson should be further respited for a period of 10 days, until Friday April 28. The newspapers that had objected to the first reprieve were unanimous in condemning the second one, the *Standard* in particular: due to the original concession to an unusual diplomatic request, the Home Secretary was now forced to respite a condemned murderer, not because he entertained any doubts concerning Lamson's guilt, but because he wanted to be civil to a foreign government.[29] The more sensible newspapers pointed out that the second reprieve was really a consequence of the first, since some of the Transatlantic documents were still not at hand. The following two days, the second and third bundles of US affidavits arrived on the *Adriatic* and the *City of Brussels*, meaning that the bulk of the American evidence could now be forwarded to the Home Office. Dr Lamson was much cheered when informed, on April 17, that his single day left to live had just become eleven full days; he remained hopeful that his father's campaign to save him from the gallows would meet with success, and that the execution would never be carried out.

*

The first affidavit came from Charles H. Nichols, medical superintendent of the Bloomingdale Asylum for the Insane in New York, who had searched the records of his institution for Lamson family members. It turned out that Dr Lamson's aunt, Caroline O. M'Gregor, a native of England but a resident of New York, had entered the asylum in 1854 at the age of 31, suffering from acute puerperal mania, and spent three years there until her death from tuberculosis in 1857. After the birth of her fourth child, she had developed hallucinosis and paranoid delusions; in the end, she had been very feeble and incoherent, taking little food and making no sense at all. Lucretia A. Lamson, the grandmother of the prisoner and a native of New York, had entered the asylum in 1863 at the age of 76, with senile dementia, and died there from general infirmity in 1867. William B. Orne, the grand-uncle of the prisoner, was a sea-captain and a native of England, but resided at Brooklyn, New York. He had entered the asylum in 1864 at the age of 87, with severe senile dementia, and died there from erysipelas and mortification of the foot after less than two months. In his *Referee* column, George R. Sims made fun of this affidavit, writing that "The American evidence of Lamson's insanity is not very strong at present. Most people's great grandmothers when they get to ninety-five are not in possession of all their faculties. If this sort of evidence is to be accepted in extenuation of cool and deliberate murder, no man ought ever to be hanged again ..."[30]

Dr Charles H. Vonklein, physician and surgeon of Hamilton, county of Butler, had served in a hospital in Bucharest that was under the direction and control of Dr Lamson. He got the impression that Lamson was possessed of a mania for treating his patients with aconitine, something that alarmed Dr Vonklein, since he knew that this drug was acutely poisonous if the dose administered was too high. He called Dr Lamson's attention to the great danger to which he subjected his patients, but the Doctor ridiculed his fears. Once, Dr Vonklein himself consulted Lamson for an attack of neuralgia, for which he was treated with aconitine in such doses that Vonklein became alarmed, although the Doctor just laughed at him. At the time Dr Vonklein had known Dr Lamson, back in 1877 and 1878, he was of the opinion that Lamson had been of unsound mind and wholly irresponsible for his conduct. Dr Francis M. Casey testified that he had met Dr Lamson in Bucharest in 1877 and 1878, and found him a very untruthful man, fond of telling yarns about his improbable wartime adventures. Several American doctors who had met Lamson in 1881 described his severe abuse of morphine and atropine.[31]

The Rev. Irving M'Elroy gave an account of Dr Lamson's visit to his household in April 1881, as did his wife Kate and sister-in-law Grace P. Williams. They gave a realistic description of the Doctor's excessive abuse of morphine and atropine, injected subcutaneously, as did Oliver L. Barbour and his two daughters, who had also met Lamson, agreeing that he had been of unsound mind due to his advanced morphine addiction. Dr William P. Hall, of Saratoga Springs, had met Dr Lamson in June 1881, and recognized him as a person of unsound mind. Dr Gustavus Winston, the New York insurance company doctor, described his failed attempt to wean Dr Lamson off the morphine in 1881. Mr Rollan M. Porter, of Potsdam, became acquainted with Dr Lamson during his stay at Rouse's Point, and often procured morphine and atropine for him at the local drug store. The addicted Doctor took it both internally and as subcutaneous injections. At time, he was violent and talked like a maniac. When he returned to London, he left behind many valuable articles that he could easily have brought with him. Dr H.H. Kane, an authority on the use and abuse of morphine, and the author of some specialist books on this subject, had never met Dr Lamson, but he pointed out that although some people could take modest doses of opiates for years without harmful effects, those of a peculiarly nervous temperament, or a hereditary tendency to insanity, could be injured out of proportion to the time the drug was taken. He rightly pointed out that hypodermic use of morphine was the most harmful. He claimed that every year, eight or nine people were admitted to the American asylums for the insane, for mental derangement secondary to the prolonged misuse of opiates.[32]

To save his only surviving son from the scaffold, the Rev. Mr Lamson was active almost around the clock, becoming increasingly desperate. He wrote two long and heartfelt letters to the Home Secretary, arguing in favour of the Doctor's insanity, and he also had Mrs Kate Lamson memorialize this dignitary, pointing out her husband's eccentric habits. As a final effort, he wrote to Queen Victoria herself, although she snubbed him, simply forwarding his letter to the Home Office.[33] The Rev. Mr Lamson also contacted his old friend Dr John Swinburne, surgeon-in-chief of the American ambulance during the Franco-Prussian war, who as we know had been fully satisfied with George Henry Lamson's work at the time. But approached by Rev. Gentleman, he completely changed his story: young Lamson had clearly been of disordered mind, and could not be trusted to administer medicines to the wounded soldiers, since he might give them a dose that was far too high. In the end, Dr Swinburne had been forced to remove Lamson from the direct care of the recently wounded, and place him in charge of the convalescents instead. Having thus perjured himself for the sake of his old friend, to save the life of the Doctor, he pointed out that his affidavit was wholly voluntary, and not asked for by any friend or relative of Dr Lamson.[34] A letter to the Home Office from 'Justice' quoted a certain Dr Crane, an American active in Paris; he knew about Dr Lamson and his valorous wartime service, as well as that Dr Swinburne had never, at the time, thought Lamson insane or irresponsible.[35]

Another witness, who identified himself as Benjamin William Brown, the coloured man of the ambulance, claimed that he had worked alongside young Lamson for 90 days during the siege of Paris. George Henry had been kind and attentive to the wounded soldiers, and very brave on the battlefield, bandaging their wounds and stabilising their fractured limbs. He had deprived himself of his own ration of horseflesh to give to the wounded. At times, he got very angry at Brown for his clumsiness and wanted to strike him 'without any reason at all'. He often gave the wounded soldiers morphine cigarettes to ease their pain, but

Brown had noticed that he was fond of smoking them himself, something that was disapproved of by the senior doctors.[36] Benjamin Meaker, verger of the American Episcopal Church in Paris, claimed to have met Dr Lamson in Paris on December 5 1881, two days after Percy had been murdered. He had urged Lamson to travel on to Florence as he had planned, although the high-minded Doctor was determined to return to London, even though his health was failing. Meaker rightly pointed out that at this time, Lamson would have had abundant opportunities to escape, with his excellent knowledge of Europe, fluent French, and good knowledge of various other languages. If he had said that he needed money, Meaker would have lent him some. This is a curious affidavit, since Meaker was never before mentioned during the protracted court proceedings against George Henry Lamson; it must be suspected that desperate to save his son, the Rev. Mr Lamson once more persuaded a witness to perjure himself.[37] The bundle of Transatlantic affidavits on the Lamson case is high on quantity but low on quality: on their cover, some Home Office dignitary has written that "there is nothing in these that we did not know before." It had already been appreciated that Lamson had been eccentric while under the influence of morphine, and it was not strange that "people would not allow him to treat them or his children."[38]

The pro-Lamson American newspapers were most enthusiastic about the last-ditch attempt of their countrymen to save the life of an American threatened with the scaffold while abroad. The *New York World* even wrote that the depositions sent across the Atlantic did not leave doubt in any impartial mind as to the diseased and irresponsible mental condition of the unfortunate Doctor; a government which puts insane men to death could not pretend to be a civilized government. The London newspapers, albeit overwhelmed by the sheer amount of material about the Doctor's morphine abuse and occasional weird behaviour, were not as excited, pointing out the cowardly nature of Lamson's crime, which he had carefully planned and executed, and the fact that during the Old Bailey trial, no mention had been made of an insanity defence. The witty George R. Sims, of the *Referee*, was not at all impressed by all these American affidavits, writing that: "The evidence of Lamson's insanity is coming over in ships from New York every day. Every ship that leaves that port for England carries something on account. The evidence itself is startling. The President of the United States has telegraphed Mr Lowell personally that he has heard from someone, whose name he forgets, that Lamson's mother-in-law's aunt had a dog that went mad, and that there is a teapot in the family that is cracked to this day. Sir William Harcourt is so affected by this evidence that he thinks of liberating Lamson on his own recognisances."[39]

★

A number of do-gooders and newspaper writers took part in the debate concerning Dr Lamson's alleged insanity. The Brompton Anti-Capital Punishment Society wrote a memorial to Sir William Harcourt, urging her Majesty "not to yield to the vulgar clamour of ignorance, malice, and prejudice, but direct a further respite in this case in order to establish the insanity of this unfortunate man, so clearly shown by his reckless use of a poison which his scientific knowledge must otherwise have taught him would have led to his instant detection."[40] The novelist Charles Reade wrote a letter to the *Daily Telegraph*, urging that the execution of Dr Lamson should be postponed for an indefinite time, for the matter of his purported insanity to be thoroughly sifted. Himself, Reade had no doubt that Lamson was insane, and that a dangerous miscarriage of justice must be prevented.[41] In his *Referee* column, George R. Sims was surprised to see Charles Reade emerge as a champion of Lamson, whom he had never met or spoken to, and found it absurd that a layperson would pretend to be able to decide on the condition of the prisoner's mind, as judged by his previous actions; he light-heartedly suggested that instead of the cumbersome procedure of trial by jury, the opinion of the President of the United States and Mr Charles Reade should be sought.[42] When the Earl of Milltown, an anti-Lamson peer, asked a question in the House of Lords whether the Home Secretary had been justified in acceding to the request from the President of the United States to respite Dr Lamson, he was answered by the Foreign Secretary Lord Granville, who pointed out that there were precedents with regard to the diplomatic representation of foreign nations interceding in ongoing criminal cases involving their countrymen.[43]

As late as April 25 and 26, further affidavits arrived via the transatlantic steamers, to be copied and forwarded to the Home Office by the solicitor Mr Mills. But on April 26, Mr Mills received a curt letter from the Home Office, containing the unwelcome news: "Sir, – I am directed by Secretary Sir William Vernon Harcourt to acquaint you that he has considered the affidavits and declarations forwarded by you respecting the case of George H. Lamson, and regrets that he can find in them no sufficient ground for advising an interference with the sentence of the law." The Doctor was doomed. There were distressing scenes when the convict Lamson was brought the dreadful news by the Governor of Wandsworth Prison, Captain Colvill; although not exhibiting much emotion, the Doctor clearly struggled hard to maintain his composure. On April 27, the London morning newspapers quoted the decision with quiet approval, one of them commenting that "The formal notification which appears in the papers this morning, that the Home Secretary finds no sufficient ground in the 'additional evidence' forwarded from America must have been generally regarded as inevitable. Lamson will therefore be hanged to-morrow, and it has been a cruel kindness which has led to such a prolongation of his suspense."[44]

When Mr Austin, from the office of the solicitor Mr Mills, had visited Dr Lamson on April 26, the Doctor had handed him a letter describing his abuse of morphine and atropine: "I did not use the first drug alone, but in combination with the latter; not, as has been supposed, to counteract the contracting effect of morphia upon the pupils of the eye, but because it not only enhanced the effects of morphia as a sedative, anodyne, and narcotic, but also because it quite, or nearly quite, overcame the sickness caused by the morphia. The habit became formed from its having been first injected hypodermically by a colleague to relieve pain. I then took it myself, having considerable work to attend to, and in order to brace myself for my professional duties while in pain. After a short time it became absolutely necessary to repeat the injections more frequently, not only for the pain, but to lull the nervous and general physical irritability, which often amounted to actual pain of a heavy rheumatic character, in the head and limbs principally, which occurred when the general effect had nearly or quite disappeared. Of course, very soon the doses had to be larger, and it required a surprisingly large amount to produce sleep, or even serious drowsiness. Usually the injection had to be repeated within three-quarters of an hour to do this, and then the sleep was of very short duration; and after the habit had existed some time it left the faculties, mental and physical, in a most peculiar and indescribable state for some hours. But the physical results, though severe and horrible to look back upon, were comparatively trifling when the moral and mental results are considered. The whole aspect became strangely and completely turned about. When in the condition above alluded to, after the narcotic effect had evanesced, the whole life was, as far as physical motions and the instincts are concerned, mechanical, and the mind full of the vaguest and most unreal fancies and imaginations. Real worries and troubles, however slight, became terrible in their awfulness, and anticipations were even more dreadful and horrible. The imagination seemed to pierce years into the future; colossal successes or failures, imaginary, would either cause a rush of warm feeling and joy, which would even cause speech to be uttered and hastening of the gait, or a despondency impossible to realize. While in the abnormal state alluded to, the most unaccountable things would be said, done, and thought of. Everything seemed one's particular right; a complete inability to draw distinction between truth and falsehood, the real and those ideals which became realities, right or wrong, a loss of the knowledge of time and distance – in fact, to a very great extent, the power of distinguishing and discriminating; a tendency, quite unconquerable, to put off things (procrastination, in a most exaggerated for and degree), my memory for names, places, and events of daily life, which was when in my normal condition unusually good, almost annulled. In all, an absolute di-naturing [sic], demoralising, dementalizing result, and withal a firm conviction that in a few days I would discontinue the habit; but the day never could come. The greatest cunning in concealing the instrument and solution, and the purchase thereof, and when used, as a rule one or two injections after going to bed, then an hour or two's sleep, then awake in that peculiar condition I have endeavoured to describe, either to get up and wander aimlessly, almost unconsciously, sometimes about the house, sometimes in the streets – those image fancies always more real at night. In New York I would rise at any hour of the night or early morning and imagine all sorts of extraordinary things I cannot now recall fully in detail – especially when President Garfield died – and stop at an all-night eating-house for slight refreshment, ice-cream and the like, and then return to my room; or else I would read, and always some highly exciting story which became at once reality to me, and then, exhausted, when nearly time for rising, would sink to uneasy sleep, fully believing I was to carry on myself the events of the narrative. When I awoke, generally another injection, a slight one, in the morning, and then one soon before getting up (which I always did very late if alone), would produce twenty to thirty minutes' half unconsciousness, and then rising, would continue the remainder of the day and evening in the state of mental absence and physical presence I have mentioned. When alone (and I always sought solitude for the greater part of the time, the presence of others in a measure interfering with the portentous and vast work the diseased brain was doing), I took neither breakfast nor lunch; but the only meal in the twenty-four hours was a late dinner, with a very little wine or beer. Whether all this was the result of morphia on the brain, always easily disturbed (delirium in the slightest illness, &c) from early years, or the effect of atropia, the effect of which I was fully and often painfully conscious of in the dryness of the throat, rendering swallowing almost impossible, and great impairment of sight from the dilated pupils, or the combination of all, I cannot say. I know these vague general outlines of the past are the results of something, and I can dimly distinguish certain acts and doings; but there were many things I did and said which were afterwards told me that I knew and know nothing whatever to my own recollection. I am firmly of the belief, vague, strange sensations existing even now, that it might be of some service were a scientific and pathological post-mortem held after my death. My relatives would probably not raise any objections to this."[45]

X.

THE END

In the morning of April 27, when the convict Lamson had just one day to live, the prison chaplain talked to him about his approaching execution, the Doctor maintaining a respectful and attentive demeanour throughout the interview. When the solicitor Mr Mills made his final visit to Dr Lamson on the afternoon, he found the convict perfectly cool and collected. He was busy writing letters to various friends, and jotting down memoranda as to how he wanted to dispose of his effects. He gave instructions to Mr Mills about certain debts due to him, which he wanted to be collected. He referred to his forthcoming execution almost with a feeling of relief, saying that anything would be preferable to the terrible state of suspense in which he had lived for the past few weeks. He seemed to view his doom with resignation and complacency, albeit being grateful for the two respites granted him, and the unceasing efforts of his father and Mr Mills to save him from the gallows. He shuddered at the thought that he would be buried in an unmarked grave inside the prison grounds, again expressing an earnest hope that a thorough post-mortem examination of his body, and most particularly his brain, would be made before burial. At half past two, Mrs Kate Lamson came to see her husband for the final time. The Doctor asked about the health of various relatives, his little daughter in particular. He told her that his fate was wholly due to his abuse of sedatives, which had rendered him almost incapable of knowing what he was really doing. Although he did his best to console her, she utterly broke down when the moment for parting arrived. As for the Rev. Mr Lamson, he had to depart for Florence posthaste, where his wife was lying dangerously ill.[1]

After seeing his wife, Dr Lamson wrote a letter to a friend who had shown great interest in his plight, in an exceedingly neat but bold hand: "My dear Mr ---, – I feel it my duty to you and all my friends, and especially to my own family and relations, to say a few words in these my last hours upon earth in reference to the offence for which I am condemned to forfeit my life so shortly. I have told you much and endeavoured to make clear to you my own impressions and ideas as to my mental and moral condition for a long time previous to the act for which I am sentenced to death. The news of my brother-in-law's death roused me as from a species of cloud; then came my long period of imprisonment at Clerkenwell; and while there necessarily the total deprivation of the drug I had so long been accustomed to. With great mental and physical suffering was the weaning accomplished, leaving, however, strongly perceptible results. Then the fearful ordeal of the trial, the awful shock of the sentence, and then the sojourn in the condemned room here face to face with death, cleared away all clouds from my mind, and now, gazing back into the mists of the past, I believe I can truly and solemnly say, as can only be said under my present conditions, that in my right and normal state of mind the compassing and committing such a crime as that for which I must now die would have been utterly and absolutely impossible and altogether foreign to my whole nature and instincts. Subject to mental disturbances from slight causes from earliest years, with a brain easily affected, the use or abuse of morphia and sedatives and narcotics made a ready physical, mental, and moral victim of me. I earnestly pray Almighty God to pardon my yielding to such habits, and trust they may be an awful warning to others similarly tempted and assailed, seeing what indescribably fearful consequences they have led in my case. I earnestly thank you and all my friends for efforts and prayers to obtain mercy for me, and, although ineffectual, you may have the great satisfaction of knowing from me that they were based upon tenable and honest grounds and foundations. Believe me, dear Mr ---, with sincerest gratitude and true friendship and regards, Most faithfully yours, Geo. H. Lamson."[2]

In the evening, the convict Lamson kept on arranging his financial affairs, writing letters to friends and arranging monetary affairs. The executioner William Marwood had come to Wandsworth Prison and inspected the scaffold and drop. He found the pit to be of insufficient depth and ordered an additional 18 inches to be dug out, but otherwise everything was in good order for the hour of death.[3]

★

1. The executioner William Marwood, from the Illustrated Police News, *December 7 1878.*

Doctor Poison

The convict Lamson had a tolerably quiet night's rest, before waking up at an early hour on April 28, destined to be his last day alive. Soon after he had risen, the prison chaplain entered the condemned cell and engaged the condemned man in devotional services, save for the interval of breakfast. At a quarter to nine, the bell of Wandsworth Prison began to toll, greatly disturbing Lamson, whose remaining minutes were counted out by that very bell. Shortly afterwards, the Under-Sheriff, the deputy-governor of Wandsworth Prison, the surgeon and four warders entered the condemned cell. The convict Lamson, who was wearing the same black suit he had worn at his trial, was allowed to walk out of the death cell between two warders at five minutes to nine, in the direction of the scaffold set up in the prison's execution shed.[4]

The procession slowly moved across the prison yard: first came two warders bearing white wands, then the prison chaplain in his surplice and hood, next the convict supported by two warders, and finally the deputy-governor and the surgeon, with several more warders. The executioner Marwood was waiting for them within the inner gates of the prison, with the straps for pinioning over his arm. When Marwood stepped forward with uplifted hand, calling out 'Halt!', Lamson staggered and almost fell against one of the warders supporting him. He trembled piteously, so badly that Marwood and the warders were fearful that he would fall down. As Marwood began to pinion him, Lamson murmured "I hope you will not hurt me." "I'll do my best not to hurt you: I'll be as gentle as I can" the humane executioner replied, as he carried on pinioning the wretched convict. One strap was buckled round the body, then the right hand was secured by another strap, and the left one by a third.

Once the convict Lamson was securely pinioned the procession moved on, the chaplain reading the service of the Church appointed for the burial of the dead, the doomed man responding almost inaudibly to the words. He was walking with great difficulty and would have fallen down had the two warders

2. *A rare 'execution broadside' on the Lamson case.*

not supported him. When he saw the scaffold and the newly dug grave next to it, he halted and almost fell, but the warders pushed him ahead and Marwood followed closely behind. As the scaffold was reached, the chaplain bade farewell to the convict, as Marwood began his preparations with the rope and the beam overhead. Anticipating that the convict Lamson would not face death courageously, the experienced hangman had put two thick planks on either side of the drop, allowing the two warders supporting the doomed man to stand securely while supporting him on the scaffold, without danger to themselves or inconvenience to the machinery of the gallows.

As the convict Lamson was forcibly kept erect while Marwood fastened his legs and put the cap over his eyes, he pitifully begged for another prayer to be recited by the chaplain, but this request was denied him. For the doomed man, life was now counted in seconds: a prayer lasted for an eternity, and a mere word would have been a welcome relief, but the hour of death had arrived for the wretched convict, just like it had once claimed the life of Percy Malcolm John. During his brief, criminous and wasted life, the Doctor had accomplished some good but also much wickedness; short and evil had been his days, as he stood on the scaffold counting one or two more seconds, the longest-lasting in his life, waiting for the drop to open. No hope. A premature tomb. The last visions of a shrouded and pinioned man. For the living, breathing, moving corpse, there was no security bell to ring inside the coffin he had constructed for himself. When Marwood drew the lever, the convict Lamson was launched into eternity; we do not know what final phantasms appeared before his eyes, not the unctuous fantasies from his father's Christian teachings, no hymn-singing angels before Peter's wicket, or the effigy of the contrite Robber on the Cross; rather the horrific phantasmagoria lurking in some of the paintings of Peter Paul Rubens, with the fallen angels tumbling to their doom in Hell, accompanied by serpents, dragons and other unclean beasts.

The chaplain finished the Lord's Prayer, in the midst of which the lever had been pulled, pronounced the benediction and moved slowly back into the prison building. The body hung for an hour, in accordance with the law, after which it was taken down and placed in a shell coffin for the purpose of inspection. Mr George Henry Hull, the very same coroner who had once conducted the inquest on the body of Percy Malcolm John, allowed evidence of identity to be procured, before Dr Wynter, the surgeon of Wandsworth Prison, stated that he had examined the body of the deceased, and that death, which had been instantaneous and painless, had been due to apoplexy. Contrary to the convict's own wishes, no autopsy was performed. The convict Lamson was buried in an unmarked grave within the prison grounds, and there his body remains to this day.

★

On April 28, the day of the execution of Dr Lamson, the London newspapers proclaimed that the previous day, he had written a definite confession that he had administered poison to Percy Malcolm John, with intent to take his life, witnessed by the chaplain and the deputy-governor of the prison, Captain L.P. Pennethorne.[5] This alleged confession was forwarded to the Home Office and is today part of their case file in the National Archives. The accompanying letter is dated May 2 1882, giving reference to a previous letter dated April 29, the day after Dr Lamson had been executed. The confession itself is dated April 31 1882, three days after the Doctor had been executed: "I, George Henry Lamson, do solemnly declare before Almighty God, that I am guilty of the murder of my brother-in-law, Percy Malcolm John, and I acknowledge the justice of the sentence passed upon men and entreat God's pardon for my crime." It is witnessed by the chaplain Mr Gilberth, and by the prison governor Captain Colvill.[6] The signature of Dr Lamson does not look genuine to me, but is likely to be written by the same person responsible for the bulk of this alleged confession. It may of course be that there is a genuine confession somewhere, but the dubious document in the National Archives file is nowhere marked 'copy', and it is a mystery where the original could have ended up.

3. *The execution of Dr Lamson, from the* Illustrated Police News, *May 6 1882.*

4. *Incidents in the Life of Marwood, from the* Illustrated Police News, *September 15 1883.*

The London newspapers reported the execution of the convict Lamson in a sombre manner, commenting that after all the uproar of the Bournemouth and American affidavits, justice had been served when such a cruel murderer perished on the gallows. George R. Sims wrote that "Lamson is dead, and his crime may be buried with him. For his relatives, his wife and his poor old father, we all have the deepest sympathy, but if he had been spared, then no one hereafter could have suffered the death penalty if there was justice in the land. ... The interference of the President of the United States was a terrible mistake. It merely prolonged the condemned man's agony. It is ridiculous to say that the Jingo spirit thirsted for Lamson's blood because a foreign Power had made itself his champion. What irritated the people was the monstrous notion that a man was to be held irresponsible for crime and cold-blooded murder because, with a full knowledge of what he was doing, he drugged himself. This plea once allowed, a man would only have to get drunk to indulge with impunity in law-breaking ad libitum. One can find sympathy for murder committed in sudden passion, but let anyone think of the prolonged and cruel agony of the helpless little cripple, let anyone picture the terrible torture the boy endured in his last hours, the torments of hell gnawing his vitals, and then speak, if he can, of the murderer in terms of pity. The action of the humanitarians is to me unaccountable. They would shriek – and rightly – against a man who inflicted on a cat such torture as Percy John endured, and yet they speak of Lamson as a poor injured sufferer, they hug him and pat him and weep over him, and say 'Poor fellow, what a shame to hang him!' Let us get capital punishment abolished, if we can; but while it is the law of the land, such wanton destroyers of life as Lamson are the last men in the world humanitarians should champion."[7]

As a high-profile London murderer, Dr Lamson was of course a prime candidate for inclusion in that unfastidious repository of criminal memorabilia, Madame Tussaud's Chamber of Horrors. The addition of his effigy was first advertised in the *Standard* newspaper of May 1, and on May 7, a newspaper could

5. *An old postcard showing Madame Tussaud's exhibition in Baker Street, once home to the wax effigy of Dr Lamson.*

announce that "A portrait model of Lamson, recently executed for the murder of his brother-in-law, Percy Malcolm John, has been added to Madame Tussaud's Exhibition." It would appear that it became quite an attraction for a while: the *Morning Post* pronounced it to be an accurate likeness, and a writer in the *Standard* exclaimed that "Lamson stood before the audience portrayed to the very life. The figure is the exact resemblance of the murderer as he stood at times during his trial at the Old Bailey."[8] When the authoress of the 'Feminine Foibles, Fancies and Fashions' column in the *Nottingham Evening Post* visited Madame Tussaud's, she "perceived among the perpetrators of the worst crimes a portrait model of Dr. Lamson."[9] But it would appear that the career of Lamson's wax effigy was not a lengthy one. On June 20, the 'London Notes' section of a provincial newspaper has an interesting paragraph: "Visitors to London who are accustomed to inspect Madame Tussaud's waxwork exhibition for the sake of the newest additions to the gallery must not expect to see in the Chamber of Horrors the figure of Dr. Lamson, the poisoner, notwithstanding the advertisements of this addition to the gallery. Dr Lamson was there for a few days, but he has disappeared mysteriously, and curious and interesting are the rumours as to the terms and conditions on which the proprietors of the show are said to have yielded to the wealthy friends of the murderer to omit this effigy from the Chamber of Horrors."[10]

One of the capsules left behind by Dr Lamson was preserved in Scotland Yard's Black Museum, inside a glass case. In 1882, CDV photographs of celebrated murderers were popular, and there was clearly one made of the Doctor, for sale to criminal enthusiasts; according to its catalogue, the Black Museum procured a copy. There is nothing about the capsule in the official catalogue of the Black Museum, but several journalists saw it at the museum in the years following the murder.[11] In 1885, a writer in *Chambers' Journal* wrote that "Under a glass shade hard by lies a gelatine capsule, a harmless-looking affair enough, but belying its appearance, for it contains a deadly poison, aconite – being, in fact the fellow to that used by Dr Lamson in 1882 to destroy his youthful brother-in-law. We are shown the carte of this criminal also, a gentlemanly looking man, by no means answering to the conventional type of assassin."[12] When an *Evening Standard* journalist was given a tour of the museum in 1889, he made a note that "Lamson's portrait is shown, a decent, pleasant faced man enough, and the fellow capsule to that with which he poisoned his brother-in-law."[13] No newspaper mentioned Dr Lamson's capsule in the Black Museum after 1890, nor is it mentioned in any book about this museum. A 1924 newspaper article about London's criminal memorabilia provides a further mystification: the capsule and the CDV and nowhere mentioned, but instead, the Black Museum boasted a small bottle of aconitine, purchased in Paris by Dr Lamson, and his original card sent to the Wimbledon schoolmaster inviting himself for an evening meal.[14] The poison was administered in a plum hidden inside a cake, the overenthusiastic journalist reported. Sadly, I am reliably informed that neither capsule nor CDV are in existence today, and the same goes for the bottle and card shown to the journalist in 1924. A fair bit of pilfering has been going on at the Black Museum over the years, surely some

6. *A newspaper photograph of Dr Lamson, perhaps identical to the elusive cabinet card image once kept at the Black Museum.*

by the very people employed to guard this valuable collection. 'Quis custodiet ipsos custodes?' would have been an apposite motto for this museum, and the individuals employed to guard it, had they been closer students of the works of Juvenal.

XI.

SOME REMAINING MYSTERIES

On June 24 1879, there had been a jolly family gathering at Horse Grove, George Henry Lamson's grand house in Rotherfield, with Kate Lamson's brother Hubert William John and sister Margaret Chapman coming to visit. Although Hubert suffered from tuberculosis, he was obviously capable of locomotion and fit enough to travel. There was tragedy when the 18-year-old Hubert died suddenly and mysteriously during this visit. Dr Lamson signed his death certificate, giving the cause of death as pulmonary consumption and amyloid degeneration, and Mrs Lamson inherited £479 in India Stocks and £269 in Consols, money that went into the Doctor's pockets.

Did Dr Lamson murder Hubert as well? As we know, he made two attempts at the life of Percy Malcolm John, using aconitine both times: the first one at Shanklin in August 1881, the second and successful one at Wimbledon in December 1881. He was clearly a person with a deficient sense of morality, and a cool and ruthless customer who was perfectly capable of murder. He had good access to poison, aconitine included, already back in 1879. The first mention of police suspicions that Hubert had also been murdered by the Doctor came in late December 1881, when there was a confused newspaper story that detectives were active in the Isle of Wight, and that the authorities were contemplating the exhumation of the body of Herbert John [his name was Hubert], who had died at Ventnor in 1870 [as we know, he died at Rotherfield in 1879].[1] No exhumation appears to have been performed, but the newspaper rumours that Hubert had not died a natural death would not go away. In March 1882, after a London morning paper had pointed out the suspicious death of Hubert in Rotherfield, the Rev. Mr Lamson and Mrs Kate Lamson indignantly denied that Dr Lamson was a double murderer: Hubert had died from 'galloping consumption', a disease extremely prevalent in the John family, several members having died from it and Mrs Lamson herself being a sufferer.[2]

In his memoirs, Montagu Williams wrote some telling words about Mrs Lamson and the mysterious death of Hubert William John: "I was very much impressed during this trial by the conduct of the prisoner's wife. She remained entirely staunch and faithful to him until the end. She had sacrificed everything in the way of money to obtain the means to defend him. Day by day a thin little figure sat half concealed behind the jury-box, and, as the public were leaving the Court every evening, at the end of the day's proceedings, this little figure would steal almost unobserved from its hiding-place, and, standing close underneath the dock, would take the prisoner's hand and kiss it most affectionately. This shows how true a woman can be, for I have but little doubt now, from many circumstances that came to my knowledge after the trial, that she full well knew her husband to be guilty. Nay, it is probable that she knew more than was proved before the legal tribunal. There can be little doubt that the other brother, Herbert [should be Hubert], by whose death Lamson came into a considerable sum of money, was also murdered by him. I am under the impression, indeed, that, before his execution, the convict made a full confession of both crimes."[3] But after the execution of Dr Lamson, the newspapers announced that although Dr Lamson had confessed murdering Percy Malcolm John, he had denied any involvement in the death of Hubert William John.[4] The alleged confession of Dr Lamson kept in his file in the National Archives does not mention Hubert John.[5]

★

Aconitine is a potent vegetable toxin produced by various noxious plants of the *Aconitum* genus, *A. Napellus* or Monkshood in particular. These plants have long had a fearsome reputation for their toxicity, but nevertheless, aconitine actually belonged to the pharmacopeia of Dr Lamson's time, as an antipyretic, analgesic and generally astringent medicine. Due to its lack of efficacy and narrow therapeutic index, it was on its way out of Western medicine already in the 1870s, however.[6]

So, why did Dr Lamson use aconitine to murder Percy Malcolm John? He may well have had experience with this drug during his wartime practice in Europe, using it as an antipyretic and analgesic preparation for the wounded soldiers, and being impressed with its toxicity. A story has been going around that during his medical studies, Lamson had been told by Professor Sir Robert Christison that aconitine was a poison that could not be traced, although forensic science had progressed since those days, with fatal results for the Doctor.[7] Robert Christison was professor of medical jurisprudence in Edinburgh from 1822 until 1832, when he became professor of medicine and therapeutics instead. He had studied under Orfila in Paris as a young man, but never had any business teaching the Paris medical students, in the late 1860s or at any other time. When Dr Lamson was brushing up his medical education in Edinburgh in 1878 before sitting his exams, Christison was 81 years old, and it is unlikely that he played any part in teaching the young doctors. Thus it is possible, but by no means proven, that Dr Lamson received, at some stage of his career, information that aconitine was a poison that could not be traced, although there is nothing to suggest that his path ever crossed that of Robert Christison.

Aconitine interacts with the voltage dependent sodium-ion channels in the cell membranes of excitable tissues, such as neurons or cardiac and skeletal muscles. Through binding to a site on a subunit of the channel protein, it keeps the sodium-ion channel open for longer, thus acting as a potent neurotoxin and cardiotoxin. The dosage of aconitine at which 50% of human beings die is just 30 μg per kilogram bodyweight, meaning that Percy would have had to ingest less than 2 mg of the poison for a fatal dose. Gastrointestinal symptoms of aconitine poisoning include nausea, vomiting, abdominal pain and diarrhoea; among the neurological symptoms are numbness and paresthesia of the face and limbs, as well as muscular weakness. It is common that the skin appears numb and 'drawn' and the throat feels constricted. The most serious symptoms are cardiovascular: hypotension, palpitations and chest pain, and particularly a variety of dangerous arrythmias, including ventricular tachycardia and fibrillation.[8] As we know, Percy had all these symptoms: his death struggle was a very painful and drawn-out process, with the eventual cause of death likely to be some kind of refractory cardiac arrythmia.

Most instances of aconitine poisoning today happen in Japan and China, where the drug is used in traditional medicine, sometimes by amateur practitioners and in excessive amounts. Furthermore, the careless Orientals occasionally mistake the monkshood for an edible plant, or eat the root thinking it is horseradish. In one instance, the plant was eaten with suicidal intent, by a young Japanese man who had a change of heart, sought hospital care, and survived. In Japan and China, aconitine is included in the standard toxicological screening used in cases of suspected herbal poisoning. Patients who do not develop cardiac arrythmia have a good chance of survival; those who do can be treated with an arsenal of effective modern antiarrythmic agents, or in severe cases with percutaneous cardiopulmonary bypass.[9]

In 1958, two Edinburgh medical students were rummaging around in a privately owned collection of materia medica. They decided to taste what they thought was a vitamin preparation, immediately experiencing a sharp, bitter taste, numbness of the face and constriction of the throat, retching and vomiting.

Although the white crystalline powder they had tasted turned out to be aconitine, both students recovered.[10] In 1996, a 61-year-old Japanese man ate an *Aconitum* plant which he thought was edible. He developed severe ventricular tachycardia and fibrillation that lasted for six hours in spite of intensive antiarrhythmic treatment in hospital, and later died of hypoxic brain damage.[11] In 2000, another careless Japanese man ate *A. napellus* thinking it was edible; after he had developed ventricular fibrillation and cardiogenic shock, he was successfully treated with cardiopulmonary bypass. After three months, he could be discharged from hospitals, hopefully also being cured of his tendency to make experiments eating unknown and noxious plants.[12] In 2003, a 17-year-old Japanese man ingested *A. napellus* with suicidal intent, developing severe refractory ventricular arrythmia that was successfully treated with a percutaneous cardiopulmonary support system.[13] In 2004, the Canadian actor Andre Noble died from aconitine poisoning after accidentally eating *A. napellus* while visiting his aunt in Newfoundland.[14]

It would take more than a century for any other poisoner to be caught murdering an enemy with aconitine. The Indian woman Lakhvir Kaur Singh was married with three children alive, but she had left her husband to enjoy a 16-year affair with another Indian living in West London, the Southall man Lakhvinder Cheema. But Cheema met a younger woman with whom he started an affair. A woman scorned, Lakhvir Singh swore that she would murder him, or burn down his house. Not long after, he ate a meal of curry prepared by her and was hospitalized for a week with what was supposed to be severe food poisoning. Lakhvir Singh travelled back to India, where she purchased a quantity of aconitine, with which she laced a refrigerated curry meal intended for the consumption of Cheema and his new paramour Gurjeet Choongh. She narrowly survived this murderous scheme, but Cheema, who had eaten the lion's share of the curry, fell ill with severe numbness of the face and paralysis of all four extremities, and expired soon after. Before his death, he had named Lakhvir Singh as the main suspect, and a lodger had seen her take the curry out of the fridge the day of the murder. A bag of aconitine was found among her belongings. On trial at the Old Bailey in 2010, she was found guilty of murder and was sentenced to imprisonment for life, with a 23-year minimum term, for the first [detected] murder with aconitine since Dr Lamson back in 1881.[15]

Hargrave Adam introduced a long-lived error when he wrote, in his introduction to the official Notable British Trials volume on the trial of Dr Lamson, that according to an unnamed person present at the trial, the Dundee cake had already been cut when brought out of the Doctor's black bag in the Wimbledon drawing-room.[16] But according to Mr Bedbrook, who had no reason to be untruthful, the cake had been brought out entire, and Dr Lamson had cut it with his pen-knife. The careless Adam went on to speculate that Lamson had 'doctored' one of the slices of the cake with aconitine and put it aside for Percy.[17] But as we know, aconitine has a very sharp and burning taste, which surely should have been discernible even to the foolhardy Percy. Moreover, it is clear from the evidence of Dr Stevenson that the cake, sweets and sherry contained no poison whatsoever. It would have made perfect sense, however, for Dr Lamson to administer the lethal dose of the aconitine hidden underneath the sugar in the capsule he handed to Percy, since this would disguise the sharp taste of the poison and delay its noxious effects until Dr Lamson had made his escape from the murder school. Yet the myth of the poisoned Dundee cake remains alive and well today, supported by careless writers who rely on Adam's account, and by a gibbering troupe of 'internet monkeys' who do their 'research' via the Google search engine.

★

When he gathered evidence in favour of his son's insanity in America and Bournemouth, the Rev. Mr Lamson welcomed every possible recruit to the cause. The argument in favour of hereditary insanity in the Lamson family is a particularly feeble one: only one of the Doctor's ancestors, namely the 31-year-old aunt Caroline O. M'Gregor, had developed an acute psychotic illness after giving birth to her fourth child. Since this 'puerperal mania' turned out to be chronic, she died insane at the asylum. The affidavit also lists two elderly Lamsons with senile dementia, but this is of little significance. Since there was probably less, rather than more, psychiatric disease among the Lamsons than there would have been in an average family, the argument in favour of hereditary insanity can be rejected.

There is evidence that George Henry Lamson became addicted to morphine during his war service in Europe, although he managed to control his use of the drug for some years to come. As late as 1878, he managed to sit a series of demanding medical examinations in Edinburgh, before purchasing a house and setting up practice in Rotherfield. Lamson had never been a particularly good doctor in civilian life: although his medical knowledge was perfectly adequate, he was indolent and inattentive, often showing his contempt for the trivial complaints presented by his patients. In 1879, his morphine addiction was getting out of control, making him careless, irritable and unreliable, and rendering his position in Rotherfield untenable. Still, he managed to achieve an orderly retreat, selling his practice and making a promising start in Bournemouth. But his addiction was progressing rapidly, with physical dependence on the drug and a variety of constitutional symptoms, including constipation, weight loss, irritability and sleep disturbance. The domestics he employed in his house thought him very odd indeed, and his Bournemouth patients were disappointed with his forgetfulness, absent-mindedness and lack of attention. He wore military decorations to which he was not entitled, made use of bogus medical degrees, and invented many falsehoods, including a libel on his friend's wife. Always a bad business man, spending vigorously on a large house well stocked with servants, he faced financial disaster as the income from his practice dropped: when the bailiffs were sent in, he fled to the United States in disgrace.

It is clear from the letters written by the Rev. Mr Lamson to Dr Gustavus Winston and the Rev. Irving M'Ilroy that at the time, he considered George Henry fully sane, although unable to wean himself off the morphine addiction that had ended his Bournemouth career. As we know, Dr Winston made an attempt to treat him, but with little success. During the Doctor's stay in London prior to the murder of Percy Malcolm John, no person suggested that he was insane and irresponsible for his actions, or questioned his ability to practice medicine. In particular, Mr Bedbrook found no symptoms of mental abnormality when Dr Lamson came calling on December 3. During his trial at the Old Bailey, for a cool and premeditated crime considered "cruel, base and treacherous" by the presiding judge, no mention was made of any insanity defence. In a letter to the *Observer*, Montagu Williams wrote that no suggestion of Dr Lamson being insane was made to him from the time the Doctor appeared at the Wandsworth police court until his conviction at the Old Bailey, a period of nearly three months. Two suggested expert witnesses had declined to go into the witness box and two character witnesses who had known Lamson abroad were never called since they did not have much to contribute.[18] George R. Sims was quite right to point out that if Dr Lamson had been considered insane, this would have opened up a dangerous legal precedent, enabling any drunkard to commit murder with impunity.[19] In a leading article, the *British Medical Journal* expressed surprise that the Lamson case had become so very protracted, with the opinion of the Home Secretary being sought concerning the affidavits collected by the Rev. Mr Lamson and the solicitor Mills. There was no doubt that Lamson had been addicted to the use of morphine for some time, and that he had taken this narcotic in excessive amounts, with pernicious and demoralising results. No convincing evidence of Lamson's mental unsoundness had been brought forward, the leader confidently declared.[20]

It is interesting to compare the Lamson case with that of the 22-year-old Mary Ann Ansell.[21] She had been working as a general servant in Bloomsbury since the age of 12, scrubbing, cleaning and washing in a dreary and menial routine. Her current employer, Mrs Margaret Maloney, thought her a decent, hard-working young woman, albeit of very limited intellect. One of Mary's duties was to receive the insurance agent John Cooper, to make sure that Mr Maloney's weekly life insurance premium was paid. One week, he suggested that she perhaps ought to insure her own life, but this she was not inclined to do. Instead, she wanted to insure the life of her elder sister Caroline, who had for some years been an inmate at Leavesden Lunatic Asylum. Mary told Cooper that Caroline worked as a servant at the hospital, and that she was in perfect health; the reason she wanted her sister's life insured was to get her a proper funeral if she died. The insurance agent agreed to insure Caroline's life for £22 10s. for a premium of a shilling per month. On March 9, Caroline Ansell received a parcel wrapped up in brown paper and marked 'London WC', containing a jam cake with an unpleasant yellow colour. Although the cake did not look particularly palatable, Caroline shared it with four other inmates. One of them took just one bite and spat it out, since it tasted queer, but the other four lunatics consumed the cake with relish. All of them soon vomited profusely, and Caroline, who had eaten the lion's share of the cake, died from jaundice and exhaustion the following day.

Since Mary Ansell did not want her sister to be cut up by the cruel doctors, her father wrote to the asylum that there was no need for an autopsy. The doctor at Leavesden found the death suspicious, however, and the coroner ordered a proper post-mortem. The findings were consistent with poisoning, and an analysis of the stomach contents showed that the poison used had been phosphorus. After Caroline's death, Mary had written to the insurance agent Cooper to claim the money, but he had declined to pay out, since Mary had told untruths about her sister's status as an asylum patient. The coroner's inquest on Caroline Ansell returned a verdict of wilful murder against her sister Mary, who was committed to stand trial at the Hertfordshire Assizes. The trial of Mary Ansell began on June 29, before Mr Justice Mathew. The newspapers described the prisoner at the bar as a coarse-looking, ugly young woman, quite tall but stooped and round-shouldered. She showed little emotion in court. For the prosecution, Mr Rawlinson QC pointed out that unbeknownst to her employer Mrs Maloney, Mary Ansell had been stockpiling phosphorus paste for an entire month. There was no doubt that this poison had been used to murder Caroline Ansell, by tricking her into eating the adulterated cake. For the defence, Mr Clarke Hall QC made much of the lack of a credible motive for the murder: was it likely that a young woman would murder her own sister for the gain of a paltry sum of money? After a hostile summing up from Mr Justice Mathew, the jury withdrew for two hours and a quarter, before returning a verdict of guilty. Commenting that never in his experience had a crime so terrible been committed for such an inadequate motive, Mr Justice Mathew sentenced her to death.

Several newspapers, the *Daily Mail* in particular, found it distasteful that a young woman should be hanged, particularly since there was a good deal of psychiatric disease in her family. All her aunts had died in asylums, her paternal grandmother had suffered from epilepsy, Caroline the murder victim had been insane and educationally subnormal, and her younger sister Martha was an imbecile. The controversial alienist Dr Forbes Winslow declared that Mary Ansell was a mental degenerate, who should not be held responsible in the eye of the law. Not entirely unreasonably, the defence was criticized for not playing the 'insanity card' in court. More than 100 MPs signed a petition urging the Home Secretary to postpone the execution to enable a further inquiry to be made into Mary Ansell's mental condition. The authorities maintained that Mary was fully sane, however, and she was executed at St Albans' Prison on July 26 1899. Mary Ansell's crime was a premeditated and dastardly one, and there were precedents that female poisoners should perish on the scaffold. Mary Ansell was clearly educationally subnormal, and she had an impressive family history of imbecility and chronic psychotic disease; it would not appear unreasonable that she did not understand the enormity of her crime. It was in her disfavour that she was a singularly unattractive person, that the *Daily Mail* was not the most respected of daily newspapers, and Forbes Winslow a busybody who was not taken seriously.

The outcome of the Lamson and Ansell cases raises the question whether any poisoner should ever be certified insane. After all, poisoning is a cruel and premeditated crime, unlikely to be committed by a lunatic. In the Lamson case, the appeal argued that the Doctor's addiction to morphine made him a person of unsound mind, but it failed since it would have set a dangerous precedent that drug and alcohol addicts could murder without paying the penalty for their crimes. In the Ansell case, the appeal argued that since the young murderess was of a very mediocre intellect, close to a mental defective, this would give her a claim to a pardon, but it failed since it would have set a precedent that mentally subnormal members of the 'criminal classes' would be able to murder people with impunity. It remains a fact, however, that the Brighton 'chocolate cream poisoner' Christiana Edmunds was pardoned from her death sentence in 1872, on grounds of insanity, but she had poisoned a boy more or less at random after first attempting the life of the wife of a doctor she wanted to marry. Like Dr Lamson and Mary Ann Ansell, she did not suffer from any chronic psychotic illness, but she does not appear to have fully understood the gravity of her crime; after spending

35 years in Broadmoor, she died there from 'senile decay' in 1907.[22] It may well have influenced the decision to pardon her that she came from a respectable middle-class family, being the daughter of an architect of some distinction. Another poisoner sent to Broadmoor was the 15-year-old Graham Frederick Young, who had poisoned his stepmother in 1962, and attempted to murder his father as well; although diagnosed as a dangerous and malevolent young psychopath, he was released after just nine years, and went on to poison two more people at a factory in Hertfordshire, just for the fun of watching them die.[23]

★

Dr Lamson's progressive morphine abuse has been outlined earlier in this book: at the time of the Franco-Prussian War, he sometimes liked to smoke the morphine cigarettes he was supposed to distribute among the wounded soldiers; he then 'learnt to like' injecting morphine hypodermically while serving in Serbia. His drug abuse was still kept under control in 1878, when he passed a series of demanding examinations in Edinburgh, with what appears to have been the greatest of ease. In the Rotherfield boredom, his abuse of morphine escalated, however, and as a result he became known as a careless and unreliable doctor. In Bournemouth, he made a good start to his medical career, but the cravings for morphine soon became too strong for him: he now seriously mismanaged both his practice and his finances, with the inevitable ruin as a result. Attempts from his father to send him to the United States for a cure did not have the desired effect, and there is evidence that while leading a vegetating existence in London planning the murder of Percy Malcolm John, he was still injecting quantities of morphine.

Morphine was first isolated from the opium poppy in 1805 and actively marketed as an analgesic medicine since 1827. In early Victorian times, the discovery of morphine was hailed as one of the great medical breakthroughs of the era: the drug was superior to all other analgetic preparations available at the time. As a result, morphine was used by both high and low, and available from grocers and tobacconists in a variety of pills and concoctions, some of them very potent indeed.[24] It was not until the Pharmacy Act of 1868 that the sale of poisons and potentially dangerous drugs was restricted to qualified pharmacists and druggists. The introduction of the hypodermic syringe in the early 1850s meant that there was now an effective method for doctors to administer morphine in an emergency. During the American Civil War, the use of morphine for wounds incurred in battle exceeded all precedents, and during the Franco-Prussian War and the Balkan wars of the 1870s, hypodermic administration of morphine was also liberally used by Dr Lamson and his fellow military surgeons.[25] At this time, morphine had also become widely used in civilian life, for the wholesale relief of pain in a variety of ailments ranging from neuralgia to cancer, without any consideration whether the patient might become addicted to the drug.

It would take until the late 1870s before there was any particular concern about the addictive potential of morphine. In an 1880 article, Dr H. Obersteiner, of Vienna, pointed out the similarities between chronic morphinism and chronic alcoholism, describing the symptoms of acute and gradual withdrawal of the drug. He claimed that "the moral degradation which accompanied morphinism, like alcoholism, may lead to actions which bring the individual into collision with the law." Three of his eight case reports concerned doctors who had become addicted to the drug.[26] In 1883, the American physician J.B. Mattison could announce that in his opinion, the majority of morphine habitués were doctors, and suggest that 30-40% of all medical professionals were addicted to the drug. In 1909, a similarly alarmist English addiction specialist claimed that medical graduates constituted 90% of all morphine addicts, and that one fifth of the mortality within the medical profession was the result of morphinism. In 1924, a German specialist estimated that 40% of all morphine addicts were doctors, and 10% doctor's wives.[27]

The observations quoted above would tend to indicate that in late Victorian times, doctors were considerably over-represented among the opium addicts. As a former military surgeon, Dr Lamson would have been exposed to the liberal use of hypodermically administered morphine from an early age, with pernicious effects. Whereas some morphine-addicted doctors managed to control their cravings for the drug, and carry on taking it in moderate quantities for decades, others of them, Lamson included, had personalities prone to progressive and severe addiction, with strong physical dependence on the drug, and progressive dementia and moral deterioration.

XII.

THE CURSE OF THE LAMSONS

After Dr Lamson had been executed, he left behind two grieving parents, a sister, a wife and a child, all of whom seems to have led singularly sad and gloomy lives after the Doctor had paid the price for his crimes. It is almost like if some malevolent supernatural entity had put a curse not only on the Doctor's remaining family, but also on various other personages involved in the case, as we will see.

The activities of Mrs Kate Lamson after her husband had been executed have remained something of a mystery for many years. The old crime writer Walter Wood had heard that Mrs Lamson had opened a boarding-house under an assumed name, and eked out the remainder of her days in obscurity.[1] Charles Kingston, another prolific old crime writer, who made it his business to investigate the fates of criminal celebrities after the verdict, found out that Mrs Lamson had opened a small boarding-house in a town sixty miles from London. Once, she was recognized there by one of the members of the Lamson jury. She died in Devonshire, still under an assumed name, and her daughter Agnes went to the United States, where she was supported by Lamson's friends and relatives, and later married a prosperous estate agent.[2]

Some research shows that these stories are falsifications, however. It has been suggested that Mrs Lamson changed her name to escape notoriety, and indeed, the 1891 Census lists a Kate G. George, aged 34 and born in Swansea, living on her own means, as a visitor to a convalescent home at No. 4-6 Westbury Road, Margate. With her was her daughter Agnes M.S. George, a scholar aged 11 and born in Rotherfield. Under her assumed name, Mrs Lamson made use of the inheritance from her two murdered brothers to take over St Michael's Convalescent Home in Westgate-on-Sea, which she would run for several years to come. It is sad but true that young Agnes Lamson, the only child of the murderer, died there on October 17 1899, aged just 20. Her death certificate curiously states her to be the "daughter of Henry George, a Doctor of Medicine (deceased)"; the cause of her death was pulmonary tuberculosis and asthenia, and her mother Kate George was present at the death.

The 1901 Census lists Kate George, a widow aged 47 and a native of Swansea, as the 'Lady in Charge of House' at St Michael's Home; there were three servants and four patients on the premises. Mrs Lamson died on December 7 1910, at Mostyn House, Ellenslea Road, St Leonards-on-Sea.[3] Her

1. *A postcard showing St Michael's Convalescent Home, Westgate-on-Sea, where Mrs Lamson lived and worked for many years, and where her daughter Agnes expired in 1899.*

death certificate describes her as the widow of Henry George, a general medical practitioner, and gives the case of death as acute bronchitis brought on by chronic pulmonary tuberculosis. The informant was her sister Margaret Chapman, of No. 43 Gordon Road, Ealing. In her will, she no longer passed under an alias: her testamentary arrangements were reported in the local newspaper without any deduction being made about her relation to the Wimbledon Poisoner of 1882. Mrs Lamson left her entire estate, net value of more than £1 701, to Margaret Chapman, her only surviving sister.

★

As for the philanthropic Rev William Lamson, father of the murderer, he became a broken man after his only surviving son had perished on the scaffold. He left Florence in 1883 and moved back to the United States, where he moved from church to church in Pennsylvania and New York, allegedly "to try to escape the memories of a son who had been murdered." In 1890, he became Rector of the Ascension Church at Bradford, Pennsylvania, but later the same year the church burnt down during the Christmas holidays, destroying all the Rev. Mr Lamson's books, papers and manuscripts. After some years, he moved on to Nyack in the State of New York, where he served as Rector at the Episcopal Church for a while, before being taken care of in a private home.

The Rev. Mr Lamson seems to have fallen upon evil times in his old age, since the *New York Daily Tribune* records that in May 1907, an old man was found wandering aimlessly around the streets of New York, pursued by a mob of men and boys who were laughing at him. At the corner of Thirteenth Avenue and 26th Street, Patrolman Kane took the old man into custody, and dispersed the mob that had been following him. The old man could not give an account of himself, but from some letters found in his bag, he was identified as the Rev. William O. Lamson, former rector of the Holy Trinity Church in Harlem, who had later held a living at Nyack, New York. He spoke confusedly about his daughter running off with an Italian nobleman, and afterwards shutting the door of her home in his face.[4] And indeed, the *New York Times* death and marriage index of 1890 mentions Julie Schuyler Lamson marrying Lieutenant A. de Filippis, of the Medical Corps of the Royal Italian Army, in Florence where her father had been working. The later life of Julia de Filippis remains a mystery: a person with that name turned up in West London from 1945 until 1950, although she does not seem to have expired in the UK.

The Rev. Mr Lamson, a shadow of his former self, explained that he had come to New York to see Bishop Potter. He was able to produce, from a small satchel he was carrying, several letters from Bishop Potter to 'The Rev. William Lamson D.D., Nyack, New York'. The Rev. Olin S. Roche, of St Peter's Episcopal Church, came to see the old man at the West 20th Street police station, but he could not get him to make much sense, except that in his old age, he was being cared for by the Rev. Dr Franklin Babbitt, Rector of Grace Church, Nyack. A doctor diagnosed him with 'paresis' and he would be sent to Bellevue on June 1, unless friends called for him. According to the *Living Church Annual*, the broken old man died in Upper Nyack, New York, on September 18, 1909.[5]

*

But what about William Henry Bedbrook, at one time the principal and proprietor of Blenheim House School? As we know, he had high hopes for his academy, and he was proud to declare that several of his boys had gone on to Oxford or Cambridge. At the time of the execution of George Henry Lamson, he was still a young man, and his prospects as an educator remained excellent. But he would not escape the Curse of Lamson, not by any means. Many parents objected to keeping their sons in a notorious murder school, and although Mr Bedbrook tried to convince them that there were no longer any murderous doctors on the premises, dosing the boys with noxious chemicals, he was soon in serious difficulties due to the lack of pupils. It did not help that there were rumours that the ghost of Percy was haunting the murder school: nervous young boys swore that they heard the whirring of the wheels of his spectral wheelchair. The murder school was still Blenheim House School in 1884, but by 1888, it had become St George's College; it was still operational as late as 1894. In the end, Mr Bedbrook had to lease the school to King's College, London, as a boarding-house for boys, but the deal was a very unfavourable one, and poor Mr Bedbrook had lost his livelihood. In 1898, he took King's College to court for allegedly breaking the original agreement, but lost his case and was condemned in costs.[6] In the end, Mr Bedbrook had to take a job as an assistant in a boot shop to provide his wife Rose and his five children with food on the table; to earn a meagre living, he sold footgear to the former pupils he had once taught Latin and Greek.[7] In the summer of 1921, when William Henry Bedbrook went bathing at Southsea, he was swept out to sea and drowned miserably. 'Famous poisoning case recalled – Aconite in Dundee Cake for Schoolboy!' exclaimed the *Dundee Evening Telegraph*, reporting on the sad demise of the 75-year-old former schoolmaster.[8] His wife Rose survived him until 1928, and he is likely to have descendants alive today.

Of the other personages connected with Blenheim House School, the assistant master Alfred Godward became an insurance clerk and died at Epsom in 1943. The pupil Walter Edward Banbury, who had been Percy's particular friend, and once visited Dr Lamson's house in Bournemouth with him, had a distinguished career as an army officer. He served in the Indian Army for many years, and then at the Western Front during the Great War, ending up a brigadier general with a CMG. Banbury retired in 1918 and died at Dumfries in 1927. As for Wimbledon's notorious murder school, it would stand for decades after Mr Bedbrook had left the premises. There were still rumours that the school was haunted by the ghost of Percy Malcolm John, and that the whirr of the wheels of his spectral wheelchair could be heard at night. In 1903, a journalist from the old crime magazine *Famous Crimes Past & Present* wanted to write a feature about Dr Lamson; he visited the murder school, of which his draughtsman left an excellent drawing, showing the outline of Blenheim House School, with its two large town houses linked with a corridor. The journalist also visited Percy Malcolm John's grave in Wimbledon Cemetery, and had his draughtsman make a likeness of it.[9] This cemetery is today the Gap Road Cemetery, and Percy is buried in lot A-A64 there, although no cross or other ornament remains today.[10]

Horse Grove in Rotherfield, home to the murderous Dr Lamson from 1878 until 1880, was taken over by his successor as the village practitioner, Dr Clarence Ellerman, but the Curse of Lamson was not yet satiated: Dr Ellerman died tragically in a bicycle accident while pedalling through Hornhurst Wood. Three other doctors followed suit as inhabitants of the house, but in 1928, the tenant of Horse Grove was Mrs Lewis Johns, a lady of quality.[11] It is strange and blameworthy that this historic house no longer stands today, and that the only remainder of the ancient Horse Grove estate in Rotherfield is the rump of a lane known as Horsegrove Lane, off New Street, which is in turn off South Street where the original house stood.

The fate of Dr Lamson's two Bournemouth properties is worthy of a short discourse. His grand detached residence 'Hursley', at the corner of Poole Road and Cambridge Road, next to the impressive St Michael's Church, was inhabited by Captain John Fowler Burbidge in the 1890s. A string of doctors and dentists followed: in 1940, the dental surgeon Mr J.K. Donald had his practice there; in 1959, a doctor and a dentist

2. The site of Dr Lamson's grand detached house 'Hursley'. Some of the original trees are likely to have survived.

were both active on the premises; in 1975, 'Hursley' was home to a firm of solicitors. In recent times, Dr Lamson's old residence has been wantonly demolished, for 'Midland House', a large and forbidding-looking office block, to be erected on the site. This disgraceful act of vandalism would seem to have satiated the Curse of Lamson, at long last.

The location of Dr Lamson's practice at No. 1 Beaumont Terrace is an interesting problem, since this terrace has long since been incorporated into Poole Hill, and the houses renumbered. It is recorded that the consulting rooms were taken over by the prominent local solicitor Henry Thomas Trevanion, who stood as a Liberal candidate in the municipal election of 1882 and lived on until 1910. There have been at least two conjectures about its situation: the Lamson biography file at the Bournemouth Library states that No. 1 Beaumont Terrace was the house immediately

3. Houses in Poole Hill, Bournemouth, including Dr Lamson's former practice at 1 Beaumont Terrace.

to the east of St Michael's Church, and the journalist Stephen Bailey put Beaumont Terrace at the present Nos. 36-46 Poole Hill.[12] A look at Steven's *Bournemouth Directory* of 1894 reveals, however, that from the Triangle to Cambridge Road, Poole Road consisted of Branksome Terrace (18 houses), Beaumont Terrace (4 houses), St Michael's Church and 'Hursley'. A Miss Milne lived in Dr Lamson's old house at No. 1 Beaumont Terrace, and she was still there in 1901. In 1914, No. 1 Beaumont Terrace is home to Mr P.W. Surplice's firm of motorcycle agents, and No. 2 Beaumont Terrace to the tailor Henry Venek; in 1923, Surplice is at No. 42 Poole Hill, as it had become, and Venek at No. 44 Poole Hill. Since the houses have not been renumbered, Dr Lamson's old practice is the present-day No. 42 Poole Hill, which has a large shop for kitchen equipment on the ground floor and two flats on the upper floors.

4. Dr Lamson's old practice today has a kitchenware emporium annexe on the ground floor. The shop is unlikely to have been there in Lamson's time.

Nor is the Isle of Wight entirely devoid of some architectural Lamsoniana. In Ventnor, the semi-detached Sydney Lodge, where the Lamson family stayed in 1871, still stands in Bath Road under its original name, enjoying fine sea views from its bay windows. When I was there, I of course tried my best to track down Clarence Villa in Shanklin, where Dr Lamson had made his first murderous attempt to end the life of the hapless young Percy. The aforementioned Mrs Maria Jolliffe is said, on her gravestone at St Blasius Churchyard in Shanklin, to have died at Clarence Villa in 1888. Her death certificate puts her place of death in St George's Road, however, and there was no Clarence Villa there in the 1930s, nor is there one today. Either the gravestone is in error and Mrs Jolliffe died at some cottage hospital rather than at Clarence Villa, or the villa has long since been pulled down. It would have made good sense for Clarence Villa to have stood

5. Sydney Lodge, Ventnor, where the Lamson family were staying in 1871, from the seaside promenade.

in Clarence Road or Clarence Gardens, but neither in the 1930s nor today was there any such house in these streets. Even an experienced murder house detective sometimes draws a blank.

★

Sir Henry Hawkins, who had presided over the trial of George Henry Lamson at the Old Bailey, retired from the bench in 1898. The following year, he was raised to the peerage as Baron Brampton, and took an active part in the debates at the House of Lords. Hale and hearty in his old age and a great friend of dogs, he published his *Reminiscences* in 1904 when he was 87 years old.[13] He died in his London house off Park Lane four years later. If Sir Henry Hawkins was spared the Curse of Lamson, the Doctor's former barrister Montagu Williams bure the full brunt of this malignant spell. In 1884, when he was just 50 years old, he began to suffer with increasing hoarseness, and was diagnosed with cancer of the larynx. In May 1886, he was operated on with a hemilaryngectomy: the entire left half of the larynx being removed. He recovered somewhat, although there was suspicion that the cancer had recurred, and was able to work as a metropolitan stipendiary magistrate for a while. He published two books of memoirs, the first of which containing a full account of his defence of Dr Lamson.[14] He died at his house in Ramsgate, from heart disease and uremia, in 1892, aged just 57. Sir Farrer Herschell, who had prosecuted Dr Lamson as solicitor-general, enjoyed a distinguished political career. He became Lord Chancellor in Gladstone's administration in 1886, and again from 1892 until 1895. He was appointed chancellor of the University of London and sat in many government commissions. In 1899, he slipped in the street, fell down hard and fractured his pelvis, dying two weeks later aged just 62. In contrast, Sir Harry Poland, who had assisted in the prosecution, led a long and fulfilling life, escaping the Curse of Lamson. He was knighted when retiring from practice in 1895, and lived on until 1928, dying in his Chelsea house aged 99.[15]

Of the various medical players in the Lamson case, Dr Other Windsor Berry carried on his practice for a few years, although the 1901 Census describes him as a 'retired doctor' living in Croydon with his family. He died in 1908, aged 64. Dr Edward Stephen Little also carried on practicing until his premature death in 1901, aged just 49. The police surgeon Thomas Bond, who had helped them conduct the autopsy, also carried on practicing for some years, writing a criminal profile on Jack the Ripper in 1888 at the instruction of Sir Robert Anderson, before committing suicide by jumping out of the window in 1901 aged 60. The Lamson case was the first one where the celebrated analyst Thomas Stevenson excelled: he was an admirable expert witness who was able to explain complex toxicological matters in a manner that the jury could understand. He took a leading forensic part in many trials involving notorious poisoners, including those of Mrs Maybrick, Thomas Neill Cream, George Chapman and Arthur Devereux. He was knighted for his services in 1904 and died of diabetes four years later, aged 70. His colleague Dr Auguste Dupré remained active as a leading analytical chemist for many years to come, although the Lamson case would remain the only one where he had appeared as an expert witness. He died in 1908 aged 72.

Chief Superintendent Frederick Adolphus Williamson continued his distinguished career after successfully solving the Wimbledon Mystery and securing the conviction of Dr Lamson. In 1886, he became Chief Constable in charge of the CID at Scotland Yard, but he died three years later aged just 59. Superintendent Charles Isaac Digby retired in the 1890s and settled down in Putney. He was a founding member of the Richmond lodge of freemasons, and lived on until 1927, when he died aged 92. Inspector James Wallis Butcher, the police detective in immediate charge of the Wimbledon Mystery, had an undistinguished further career: the Lamson case would remain his only major murder investigation. He died in 1900, aged 64.

6. *Sir William Stevenson in his old age, from* Vanity Fair, *November 30 1899.*

Of the Bournemouth people involved in the Lamson case, the estate agent Edward Wyse Rebbeck, who once instructed the bailiffs to evict the Doctor from 'Hursley', did very well for himself and became a wealthy capitalist; he was still living in Bournemouth in 1911. Price Owen, whom Dr Lamson once cheated out of £20 with a dud cheque, was also still living in Bournemouth in 1911, as a retired wine merchant. Of the Londoners who had the misfortune to cross the Doctor's path, the two pharmacy assistants William Ralph Dodd and Charles Ernest Betts both continued their humble careers after giving evidence in the Lamson trial; in 1911, Dodd was a manufacturing chemist in Edmonton. In contrast, Dr Lamson's old friend, the hard-drinking medical student John Law Tulloch, never graduated from medical school, and disappeared into obscurity. Finally, the Doctor's particular foe, the hotel-keeper James Creighton Nelson, did of course not survive the Curse of Lamson very long: he died already in 1885, aged 64.

XIII.

SUCH DEADLY DOCTORS

William Palmer was born in Rugeley, Staffordshire, in 1824, the sixth of eight children of the wealthy sawyer Joseph Palmer and his wife Sarah. His father died when he was 12 years old, and his mother cashed in a handsome inheritance. Young Palmer received a decent education at the local grammar school, before being apprenticed to a Liverpool chemist. He was dismissed after stealing money, however, and his wealthy mother had to repay his employer all the missing funds to make sure that he avoided criminal prosecution. He was then apprenticed to a local doctor, but once more got into trouble after money went missing and a number of servant girls were put in the family way. Mrs Palmer paid for him to go to London and study medicine at St Bartholomew's Hospital, where he ultimately graduated as a Member of the Royal College of Surgeons in August 1846.

Dr Palmer returned to Rugeley and went into practice at his house in Market Square. He married Ann Thornton in 1847. His mother-in-law, a hard-drinking old woman, came to visit them in early 1849; after she had died mysteriously, Palmer and his wife were in for a handy inheritance. The couple had five children, of whom the eldest son survived his father, but all the other children died at an early age. William Palmer appears to have been a competent enough doctor, albeit idle and lazy; his main interest in life was betting on the horseraces. He built up his own stable of horses and travelled extensively to various racing events. In 1850,

Doctor Poison

1. *A portrait of Dr William Palmer, from G.H. Knott (Ed.), Trial of William Palmer.*

he borrowed money from a man named Leonard Bladen, who died mysteriously in Palmer's house shortly afterwards; it attracted notice that in spite of having won at the races, he had very little money on him, and that his betting books were nowhere to be found. Palmer signed the death certificate himself, with the diagnosis of an abscess of the pelvis.

Dr Palmer kept gambling hard and frequently lost. To recoup his failing fortunes,

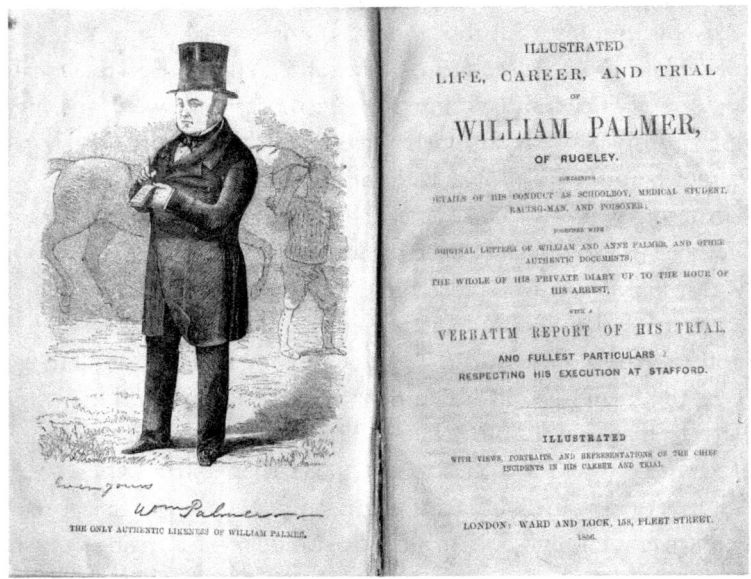

2. *An old 'Trial' with a portrait of Dr Palmer.*

he took out a £13 000 life insurance policy on his wife, who died soon after from what was believed to be cholera. He also kept forging his wealthy mother's signature to pay off creditors. When two of the creditors were pressing to get their money, and threatening to speak to Mrs Palmer, the wily doctor took out a life insurance on his brother Walter, a drunk who was liberally supplied with gin and brandy so that he would drink himself to death. But when Walter died soon after, the insurance company refused to pay up. This was a hard blow for Dr Palmer, who had been enjoying an affair with the housemaid Eliza Tharme that resulted in the birth of an illegitimate son, and further expenses for him.

One of William Palmer's horseracing associates was James Parsons Cook, a sickly and hard-drinking young man who had inherited £12 000. In November 1855, they attended the Shrewsbury races: the fortunate Cook won £3 000 but Palmer lost heavily. Not long after, Cook complained that his gin tasted

3. A postcard showing the effigy of Dr Palmer in Madame Tussaud's now defunct Chamber of Horrors.

uncommonly strong and burnt his throat; when he was violently sick, he said "I believe that damned Palmer has been dosing me!" Nevertheless, the foolhardy Cook accompanied Palmer to Rugeley a few days later, where he took a room at the Talbot Arms. He was soon sick again after Palmer had bought him some gin; a servant maid fell ill after tasting some of the drink, but Cook still kept swigging from the bottle, in between vomiting. The following day, Palmer began collecting money from bets won by his 'friend' Cook, to the tune of £1 200. He then purchased strychnine and ammonia and administered it to the drunken gambler, who died in agony. Dr Palmer made sure that an 80-year-old doctor signed a death certificate with 'apoplexy' given as the cause of death, and that the post-mortem, where he himself assisted and took away the stomach contents, was badly bungled. Following a pattern that the reader will recognize, Cook's betting books mysteriously disappeared, and Palmer pocketed £4 000 in outstanding medical fees.

4. Dr Palmer's house in Rugeley, from an old postcard. The house is still standing today.

But although the bungling of the autopsy meant that there was no forensic evidence that Cook had been poisoned, the circumstantial evidence against Palmer was such that the coroner's inquest returned the verdict of wilful murder against William Palmer. Since it was believed that a fair jury could not be found in Staffordshire, the trial was held at the Old Bailey. The body of Ann Palmer was exhumed and found to contain antimony, but the body of Walter Palmer was too badly decomposed for any analysis to be made. Despite being ably defended by Mr Serjeant Shee, the evidence against Palmer was overwhelming. With his precarious financial position, he was desperately in need of money, two chemists had sold him strychnine before the murder, and on his death-bed, Cook had accused Palmer of murdering him. Dr Palmer was found guilty of murder, sentenced to death, and hanged in front of 30 000 spectators at Stafford Prison on June 14 1856.[1] His wax effigy stood at Madame Tussaud's from 1856 until it was removed in 1979.

★

Edward William Pritchard was born in Southsea, Hampshire, on December 6 1825, the son of Captain John White Pritchard RN. He had at least three brothers, of whom one rose to become secretary to the naval commander-in-chief at Plymouth, and another became a staff surgeon in the Royal Navy; there were also at least three sisters, who all married. After schooling in London and Paris, Edward William was apprenticed to two Portsmouth surgeons, before qualifying as a Member of the Royal College of Surgeons in 1846. He was gazetted assistant surgeon in the Royal Navy later the same year, and went on to sail the seven seas, in different ships, for nearly five years. In 1850, when he was serving on board the *Hecate* at Portsmouth, Edward William met the respectable Edinburgh heiress Mary Jane Taylor, and they married after a short acquaintance.

5. *A photograph of Dr Pritchard, from W. Roughead (Ed.), Trial of Dr Pritchard.*

In 1851, Edward William Pritchard purchased a medical practice in Hunmanby, Yorkshire, and moved into Warburton House in the village centre [it still stands] with his wife. He soon had four children alive: Jane Frances, Charles Edward, Horatio Michael and William Kenneth, as well as the daughter Zillah Catherine who died young. He became known as a competent doctor, who wrote a number of case reports and letters to the contemporary medical press, as well as a guide-book to the local watering resort of Filey. He was an active Freemason and a keen member of the local Temperance Society, which he harangued more than once, pointing out the evil of Demon Drink. Dr Pritchard was always well dressed, and he was thought of as something of a ladies' man. He grew a large bushy beard, and made vain attempts to disguise his balding head by combing what remained of his long hair over it. In character, he was conceited and boastful: he tended to exaggerate his travelling exploits as a young naval surgeon, and some of the books he claimed to have written do not appear to exist.

In 1857, Edward William Pritchard acquired, by purchase, the title of MD from the University of Erlangen in Germany. The following year, he passed another examination to become a Licentiate of the Society of Apothecaries on London. He then sold his practice in Yorkshire and accompanied a wealthy gentleman to the Holy Land, as his medical advisor, having sent his wife and children away to the Taylor family home at No. 1 Lauder Road in Edinburgh [it still stands]. After his return from abroad, Dr Pritchard set up practice at No. 11 Berkeley Terrace, Glasgow [today No. 66 Berkeley Street; it still stands]. The dour local doctors were far from impressed with this flashy interloper from south of the border, but although he remained fond of telling tall stories, like having plucked eaglets from their eyries in the deserts of Arabia and hunted mountain lions in America, and equally fond of chasing the ladies in spite of his large family, the bonhomous Dr Pritchard managed to stay afloat. After all, he was a fully competent doctor, capable of holding his own in the competitive Glaswegian medical world. In May 1863, there was a mysterious fire at No. 11 Berkeley Terrace, in which a young servant girl in Dr Pritchard's employ lost her life; it was presumed by some that Pritchard had sedated her after she had become pregnant with his child, and then set her room alight, but this suspicion was not pursued by the authorities at the time.

6. *Dr Pritchard's house at No. 131 (later No. 249) Sauchiehall Street, Glasgow, from W. Roughead (Ed.), Trial of Dr Pritchard. The house no longer stands, having been wantonly demolished in quite recent times.*

Soon after the fire, Dr Pritchard moved to No. 22 Royal Crescent in central Glasgow [the house is today a hotel] with his family of five children; the youngest daughter Elizabeth having been born in Glasgow in 1860. In 1864, the family moved again, to a house in Clarence Place, Sauchiehall Street [later No. 131 Sauchiehall Street, renumbered as No. 249; wantonly destroyed in relatively recent times, for the construction of a kitchenware emporium]. But by this time, all was not well with the Pritchard family. The hard-spending Dr Pritchard was constantly short of cash, so the purchase of the house and practice in Clarence Place, from a certain Dr Corbett, had to be financed with a heavy mortgage, and a loan of £500 from Pritchard's wealthy mother-in-law Mrs Jane Cowper Taylor. Furthermore, the womanizing doctor had seduced his 15-year-old maidservant Mary McLeod, having to perform an abortion when she became pregnant. In a weak moment, Pritchard promised that he would marry young Mary if something happened to his wife.

Edward William Pritchard had by this time grown tired of his wife, who had lost her looks after six pregnancies in quick succession. He was well aware of his overdrawn bank accounts, and of the very healthy state of the finances of his wife's family. Dr Pritchard built up a stockpile of poison, and started dosing his wife with increasing doses of antimony; when she was removed to the family home in Edinburgh, she improved markedly, but only to deteriorate again once back at Clarence Place. As for the annoying mother-in-law, she came to visit on February 25 1865, hungrily eating a tapioca pudding which Pritchard had 'doctored' with a lethal dose of Fleming's Tincture of Aconite; after she had collapsed and expired, Pritchard himself signed her death certificate, attributing the death to a stroke. When Mrs Pritchard herself died on March 18 the same year, her husband registered the death as caused by gastric fever. But the deaths of his mother-in-law and his wife, in quick succession, under Dr Pritchard's own roof in Glasgow, had not gone unnoticed by his professional rivals, and the procurator-fiscal received an anonymous letter from one of them, accusing Pritchard of being a double murderer. This letter was taken seriously: Dr Pritchard was promptly arrested to prevent his escape, and care was taken to examine the bodies of the two deceased women for poison.

After large quantities of poison had been detected in the bodies of both the murdered woman, Dr Pritchard had to stand trial for murder before the high court of justiciary in Edinburgh. The defence suggested that Mary McLeod was the guilty woman, but they were not believed. The prosecution provided solid evidence about the sad state of Pritchard's finances and the hefty sum he would receive once the two women were dead; the druggists had recorded his purchase of poison in their books, so that it was definitely proven that prior to the two poisonings, Pritchard had been stockpiling antimony and Fleming's Tincture. At long last, the cowardly doctor confessed his guilt, clearing his conscience and exonerating Mary McLeod. He was hanged by William Calcraft in front of Glasgow Prison on July 28 1865, with 100 000 people attending what would be the last public execution in Glasgow.[2] Dr Pritchard's sons Horatio Michael and William Kenneth became master mariners; since they both married, and the former of them had issue, there are still living descendants of Pritchard the Poisoner in the United States today.

★

Thomas Neill Cream was born on 27 May 1850 at No. 61 Wellington Lane in central Glasgow, the son of the clerk William Cream and his wife Mary. William Cream had higher hopes for his future than clerking in Glasgow, however: in 1854, he emigrated to Canada, where he became manager of a major Quebec shipbuilding and lumber firm. Young Thomas attended school in Quebec and became an apprentice at a shipbuilding firm. But due to his father's undoubted success, he could set

7. *A photograph of Dr Neill Cream, from W. Teignmouth Shore,* Trial of Neill Cream.

his sights higher: in 1872, he became a medical student at McGill College in Montreal, returning to Quebec each summer to work for his father. In March 1876, he passed some kind of intermediary medical exam, defending a thesis on the effects of chloroform. A wild young fellow, he was suspected of setting fire to his rooms the following month, in order to collect the insurance money. Then there was the matter of young Flora Brooks, daughter of a respectable hotel owner in Waterloo, a town south of Quebec: she was seduced by Thomas Neill Cream, and fell ill after he had performed an abortion on her. Her enraged father dragged Cream back to Waterloo and forced him to wed Flora in a shotgun marriage, before the unwilling bridegroom skulked off to continue his medical studies in London, leaving Flora behind.

Arriving in London in October 1876, Thomas Neill Cream attended medical lectures in between courting young ladies, making slow but steady progress through the curriculum. In April 1877, he failed the anatomy and physiology examinations at the Royal College of Surgeons, a disgrace that made him concentrate on his studies for a while and leave his lady friends alone. He was cheered to find out that his wife Flora had died mysteriously back in Canada, and claimed a thousand dollars from his father-in-law, eventually settling for two hundred. In April 1878, he was admitted to the Royal Colleges of Physicians and Surgeons of

Edinburgh, with an additional license in midwifery. Although he now had a right to practice medicine in Britain, Thomas Neill Cream returned to Canada in May 1878 and set up a practice in London, Ontario, specialising in obstetrics and gynaecology. But the following year, Kate Gardener, one of Cream's patients, was found dead near his practice, from an overdose of chloroform during an abortion. At the inquest, it was clear that Cream had had been the abortionist. There were allegations that he had offered money to Kate Gardener if she took part in a blackmail plot, accusing a wealthy man of being the father of her unborn child. Another doctor made it clear that the suspicious death of Kate Gardener could hardly have been suicide, since she would have been unable to hold the chloroform-soaked sponge to her nose for long enough. The ruling of the inquest was that of murder against some person unknown, although Cream was hounded out of Canada with rapidity, as an abortionist, suspected blackmailer and possible murderer.

Thomas Neill Cream took refuge in Chicago, a city where he presumed scoundrels could thrive and be happy. He obtained a medical license and started a practice as an obstetrician once again. He soon became known to the police as an abortionist. But in August 1880, the decomposing remains of the young woman Mary Anne Faulkner, of Ottawa in Canada, were found inside the apartment of Hattie Mack, a young Afro-American midwife who sometimes assisted Dr Cream. It soon became clear that both Cream and Mack had been involved in her untimely death after a botched abortion, but the suave Dr Cream made a good impression in court, whereas the foolish woman Mack lied and prevaricated. In the end, Cream got off scot-free to continue his criminal career. In early 1881, he tried to blackmail the druggist Frank Pyatt for causing the death of Ellen Stack, one of Cream's own patients, but he was never prosecuted. Cream then tried to blackmail his patient Joseph Martin, claiming that he had never paid his bills, and that he had infected his wife and children with venereal disease. In April the same year, a woman named Alice Montgomery died of strychnine poisoning following an abortion, not far from Cream's practice. This all-rounder in crime next seduced Mrs Julia Stott, the much younger wife of an old stationmaster who suffered from epilepsy. Cream prescribed some medicine for old man Stott, who died mysteriously in July 1881. This time, the authorities acted with more alacrity: although Cream had tried to implicate another Chicago druggist in the poisoning of Daniel Stott, he was charged with murder. The medicine he had provided for Stott contained strychnine, and forensic analysis of the stomach of the dead man indicated that he had been poisoned to death. Cream tried to escape to Canada, but was apprehended and brought back to Chicago, tried and convicted of murder, and sentenced to be imprisonment for life. The only reason he had not been sentenced to death for his callous and cowardly crime was that the part played by Mrs Julia Stott, a woman of indifferent morals who had uttered threats against her husband.

The sturdy doors of the Illinois State Penitentiary at Joliet closed behind Thomas Neill Cream. The keys were thrown

8. Features on the Neill Cream case, from the
Illustrated Police News, July 9 1892.

away. This dismal prison was to become his home for the next 10 years. But in 1891, Cream's brother Daniel approached the Governor and succeeded in getting the murderer out of prison, as a proper subject for executive clemency. Prison had toughened up the once dapper medical man, and made him a foul-mouthed thug, addicted to drugs and capable of anything. Because his medical knowledge had of course not benefited from his long stay behind bars, he was no longer capable of practicing. Since he had inherited $16 000 from his father, who had died while he was 'inside', he felt no inclination to do any work. In October 1891, he travelled back to London, where he took a room at Lambeth Palace Road, right in the middle of the red-light district south of the river. He visited the local druggists and built up a stockpile of strychnine and other poisons. On October 13, the young prostitute Nellie Donworth accepted a drink from Dr Cream. A few days later, she died from strychnine poisoning. During the inquest, Dr Cream wrote to the coroner, offering to name the murderer for a £300 000 reward. He also wrote an anonymous letter to W.F.D. Smith, owner of the W.H. Smith bookselling chain, accusing him of committing the murder and demanding money for keeping silent about it. On October 20, he met the prostitute Matilda Clover, who fell ill and died the following day, from what was presumed to have been the DTs. Dr Cream wrote an anonymous letter to the physician Dr William Broadbent, accusing him of murdering her and demanding money for keeping quiet, but Broadbent forwarded the letter to Scotland Yard. In between murdering prostitutes and making unsuccessful attempts at blackmail, Thomas Neill Cream also had time to get himself a girlfriend, the respectable dressmaker Laura Sabbatini, whom he was supposed to marry after going for a visit to Canada to take care of his father's estate.

Thomas Neill Cream left for Quebec on January 7 1892, drinking hard on the way and taking morphine pills to be able to sleep. He had brought with him a collection of pornographic photographs, which he showed to the less fastidious fellow travellers. Daniel Cream's wife found him such a sinister presence that she forced him to stay at a hotel rather than in the Cream family home. On April 2 1892, Thomas Neill Cream was back in London, where he continued his murderous career. On April 11, he picked up the young prostitutes Alice Marsh and Emma Shrivell, and went to their flat where he poisoned them with some bottles of Guinness laced with strychnine. Since he kept writing blackmail letters to various people, he was soon in trouble, however, since he had referred to the murder of Matilda Clover when her death had in fact been ascribed to her alcoholism. The police realized that the letter writer who had been pestering people was most likely the Lambeth Poisoner himself. When a New York policeman met the bonhomous Dr Cream, he was taken for a guided tour of all the murder sites, something the Scotland Yard detectives found suspicious. They found out that Cream was in the habit of visiting prostitutes, that he had employed Laura Sabbatini to write blackmail letters from his dictation, and that he was a convicted murderer in the United States. He was arrested on June 3 and charged with quadruple murder. A prostitute named Lou Harvey came forward to say that Cream had given her some pills for her complexion, but she had become suspicious and just pretended to swallow them, later throwing these lethal pills into the Thames.

On trial at the Old Bailey on October 17 1892, before Sir Henry Hawkins, the evidence against Thomas Neill Cream was rock solid. The jury was out for just 12 minutes before returning a verdict of guilty on all four counts of murder. Cream was hanged at Newgate on November 15, by the executioner James Billington.[3] There has been a curious legend that on the scaffold, his last words had been 'I am Jack the ...'. But although there has been speculation about look-alikes taking the place of the imprisoned murderer, or that he used a bribe to get free already in 1888, there is solid proof that Cream was incarcerated in Joliet Prison during Jack the Ripper's Autumn of Terror back in 1888. In a newspaper article, the strange coincidences between Dr Lamson and Dr Cream were commented upon. Both were transatlantic types and both were medically qualified, although

9. *The execution of Dr Neill Cream, from the* Illustrated Police News, *November 19 1892.*

only Lamson practiced medicine in Britain. Both were in the habit of travelling between Britain and the United States or Canada. Dr Thomas Stevenson, who had proved the presence of aconitine in the organs of Percy Malcolm John, was the analyst who proved the presence of strychnine in the body of Matilda Clover, testing it by injecting an extract and killing a frog. Just like Lamson had willingly gone to Scotland Yard after reading about his suspected involvement in the murder in the newspapers, the brazen Cream had gone to the police to complain about being shadowed by the detectives. Both had been charged in the small upstairs court at Bow Street, and both had been incarcerated in Cell No. 8 there. Chief Superintendent Frederick Adolphus Williamson had been the police detective in charge of the Lamson investigation; it was his son, who had become a treasury solicitor, who helped present the evidence against Cream at the inquest on Matilda Clover.[4]

★

10. *A photograph of Dr Crippen.*

Hawley Harvey Crippen was born in Cold Water, Michigan, in 1862, the son of a dry goods merchant. He studied medicine, obtaining a MD degree at the Cleveland Hospital College, and later worked as an aurist and oculist in various cities, often as an assistant to more senior and successful doctors. He married Charlotte Bell in 1887 and they had a son named Otto. In 1893, after his first wife had died, Dr

Crippen met the pretty and vivacious 17-year-old Cora Turner, a kept woman who was being attended by the New York doctor whom he served as assistant. The 31-year-old Crippen fell in love with her and they married after a few weeks. One day she told him that her real name was Kunigunde Mackamotzki, and that her father was a Pole and her mother a German. Crippen's reaction to this singular announcement has not been recorded. When 'Cora' wanted to train as an opera singer, Crippen paid all her expenses. The problem was that his own medical career had failed to take off: he could not establish a practice and had fallen in with an undesirable crowd of quacks and homeopathists. For a while, he even prescribed homeopathic medicines via mail order to patients who wrote letters to the patent medicine company describing their symptoms.

In 1900, Dr Crippen moved to London, where he would work as the sales representative to various American patent medicine companies. Although he could still call himself 'Doctor', his American degree gave him no licence to practice in Britain without sitting a series of difficult exams in London or Edinburgh, something he was not up to with his limited and outdated medical knowledge. Anyway, he probably did not miss his patients much, preferring a steady job selling patent remedies. Cora joined him in London after a while, when her hopes of a New York operatic career had come a cropper. She wanted to become a star in the London music halls instead, and in spite of Dr Crippen's objections, Belle Elmore, singer and performer, made her grand debut not long after. But since she lacked both voice and talent, and since there were many better and more attractive music hall artists at the time, her engagements were few and far between. Understandably, this state of affairs frustrated her a good deal, and she sometimes quarrelled bitterly with her husband, who wanted her to stay at home and look after the household. The contrast between this mismatched couple could hardly have been greater: she was a florid, sturdy dame, much given to histrionic outbursts; he was a quiet little man with a balding head, strong spectacles and a large drooping moustache. In 1905, the two Crippens moved into the capacious semi-detached house at No. 39 Hilldrop Crescent, Holloway. As the years went by, the state of their marriage steadily deteriorated: Crippen suspected that Cora was having an affair with the American music hall artist Bruce Miller, and she was suspicious of Crippen's young typist Ethel Le Neve, who seemed very friendly with her employer.

In June 1910, two of Cora Crippen's theatrical friends went to alert New Scotland Yard about the mysterious disappearance of 'Belle Elmore'. She had last been seen holding a dinner party with her husband on January 31. Dr Crippen had later said that she had left him to join Bruce Miller in the United States, adding that she had caught a chill and died from pneumonia in Los Angeles six weeks later, but Cora's friends did not believe him. They knew that Ethel Le Neve was now living at No. 39 Hilldrop Crescent, and one theatrical lady had seen her at a party, wearing one of Cora's distinctive brooches. Detective Chief Inspector Walter Dew, one of Scotland Yard's foremost detectives, went to see Crippen at his home on July 8, with his sergeant in tow. The guilty pair at No. 39 Hilldrop Crescent were probably quite alarmed to have two police detectives come calling, although the suave Dr Crippen made use of his best

11. A postcard showing Dr Crippen and Ethel Le Neve in the dock.

bedside manner to explain how his faithless wife had run away to America to join her lover there. The story he had told Cora's theatrical friends, namely that she had expired from pneumonia, had been a falsehood, he confessed, but he had no idea where she was at the present time. It attracted suspicion that Crippen was clearly a very dodgy kind of doctor, without both patients and practice, and earning his living by peddling quack medicines. There was also an obvious motive for Crippen to get rid of his wife, namely that Ethel Le Neve was living in sin with him at his house.

On July 11, Chief Inspector Dew returned to challenge Dr Crippen and Ethel Le Neve, but the guilty pair were nowhere to be found. It turned out that twelve hours after Dew's initial visit, Crippen and Ethel had made haste to leave London. Since this was of course indicative of their guilt, the detectives returned to No. 39 Hilldrop Crescent, to search the house properly this time. Lifting the bricks that formed the floor of the coal cellar, they found a quantity of putrefied human flesh. Although the head, limbs, bones and genitals were missing, Dew felt certain that these dismembered remains represented the grisly end of Cora Crippen alias Belle Elmore. The experienced detective also suspected that the canny Dr Crippen was heading back to the United States via some stratagem or other, but since there were many seaports and an abundance of transatlantic liners, it might prove difficult to track him down. The full description of Dr Crippen and Ethel Le Neve was widely circulated in the newspapers, and the manhunt was on.

One of the mariners who read the description of Dr Crippen and Ethel le Neve was Henry Kendall, captain of the steamship 'Montrose', sailing from Antwerp to Canada. Kendall took an interest in a mystery American passenger who called himself John Philo Robinson, and who was travelling with his young son. When Kendall saw the 'son' squeeze Robinson's hand in an intimate manner, he found it quite unnatural. He got hold of a newspaper appeal about Dr Crippen and saw that although 'Robinson' had shaved off his tell-tale moustache, discarded his glasses and grown a short beard, he was clearly identical to the fugitive doctor. The 'son' was of course Ethel Le Neve in male attire and with her hair cropped short. Kendall instructed his Marconi wireless operator to send a message to Scotland Yard that he had strong suspicion that Dr Crippen and Ethel Le Neve were on board his vessel. Chief Inspector Dew was dispatched to Canada on a faster ship, where he managed to apprehend the fugitive doctor and his paramour, without any drama, and bring them with him back to London.

There was immense newspaper interest in the Crippen case: the sordid murder story became a thrilling drama, the unprepossessing little doctor a great murderer for the sake of love, and the drab Ethel Le Neve a romantic heroine. On trial at the Old Bailey, things were not looking good for Dr Crippen. Cora had disappeared, without ever being seen again, and left her beloved jewellery and furs behind. Human remains had been found in the cellar of No. 39 Hilldrop Crescent, some of them wrapped in Dr Crippen's pyjamas. Hair and curlers identified as resembling those possessed by Cora were found among the remains. The remains contained the poison hyoscine, purchased by Crippen shortly before Cora's disappearance, and never accounted for. The remains were covered in lime, purchased by Dr Crippen prior to the murder. Nor was it of course the action of an innocent man to leave his house and his job without notice, pawn Cora's jewellery, and travel abroad in disguise and under an assumed name, taking with him his mistress disguised as a boy. Although ably defended by Mr Alfred Tobin, the evidence against him was overwhelming; the jury was out for just 27 minutes before returning a verdict of guilty, and Crippen was sentenced to death and hanged by John Ellis at Pentonville Prison on November 23 1910.[5] His wax effigy was on display at Madame Tussaud's for many years, having been saved from a flooding incident in

1925 and repaired after losing its head in an earthquake in 1931, until the Chamber of Horrors was closed down in recent years. As for Ethel Le Neve, she was charged with being an accessory after the fact but acquitted; she later married a man named Smith and died in Dulwich in 1967, having managed to keep her past a secret for decades.

For many years, rumours have been circulating that Dr Crippen was innocent. At first, there were alleged sightings of Cora all over the world, and dubious anonymous letters claiming that she was living a comfortable life in

12. Dr Crippen in the dock, a postcard showing the effigy from Madame Tussaud's Chamber of Horrors.

the United States, having left her unfaithful husband to perish on the scaffold. Might the human remains at Hilldrop Crescent not have belonged to a patient killed misadvertently by Crippen during an abortion, it was asked, but there was never anything to indicate that the mild-mannered doctor ever had any feticidal ambitions, or that he saw patients in his house. In 2007, the arguments in favour of Crippen's innocence were reviewed in the Channel 5 documentary *Revealed: Was Crippen Innocent?* Albeit marred by the sensationalism inherent in such TV productions, the documentary made a good job of casting doubt on the 1910 conviction. The prime mover behind it was the American forensic scientist John Trestrail, who had long taken an interest in the case. He had made sure that mitochondrial DNA from a microscope slide of tissue from the human remains found at No. 39 Hilldrop

Crescent was compared with that from alleged blood relatives of Cora Crippen in the female line; they did not match. Moreover, the tissue came from a male! In a scholarly article published in 2011, Dr Trestrail and his colleagues expressed themselves with praiseworthy moderation, but the TV documentary makers boldly alleged that there had been a conspiracy: in order to get Crippen convicted, Chief Inspector Dew had procured a male cadaver, butchered it, added some hyoscine and the pyjamas, and planted the remains in Dr Crippen's coal cellar.[6] But for such a conspiracy to have the desired effect, the detective must have been absolutely sure that Cora Crippen would not turn up in the United States, as her husband had suggested that she might. Moreover, Walter Dew was known for his honesty and integrity, and it is quite unthinkable that he would falsify evidence in such a manner. It is more likely that the tissue on the microscope slide had been contaminated, since there is evidence that it had been handled by many people back in 1910, with poor hygienic standards. Today, such handling of a specimen would have made the DNA result inadmissible as evidence. In December 2009, the Criminal Cases Review Commission reviewed the case and turned down a request to have the Court of Appeal decide whether to pardon Crippen posthumously.

As for the murder house at No. 39 Hilldrop Crescent, it was next occupied by the Glaswegian comedian Adam Arthur, who called himself Sandy McNab. He renamed it 'McNab House' and had two postcards printed of himself standing by the gateposts, which had been adorned with Scottish thistles. In November 1910, he told the readers of *Thomson's Weekly News* all about his experiences in London's most recent murder house. He wanted to open the house to the public as a museum with various Crippen relics, but since this was thought in very poor taste, it became theatrical lodgings instead. In 1914, McNab was arrested as a paedophile after sexually assaulting a 13-year-old girl; he was imprisoned for two years, and the Crippen murder house passed

13. Dr Crippen's house at No. 39 Hilldrop Crescent, which was bought at a discount price by the comedian Sandy McNab after the doctor had been executed. The house was demolished in the 1950s due to wartime structural damage.

on to new owners. In 1940, a Luftwaffe bomb landed in the back garden of No. 40 Hilldrop Crescent, the subsequent explosion damaging the rear of the adjoining houses severely, causing structural instability. Dr Crippen's house was finally demolished in 1951, along with Nos. 37-40; a nondescript modern block today stands on the site. A council proposal to adorn this building with a blue plaque, thanks to its indirect association with Crippen, was not acted upon.

★

Bukthyar Rustomyi Hakim was born into a respectable Parsee family in Bombay, on March 21 1899. He received a good education, and qualified as a doctor at the local university in 1922.

14. *A photograph of Dr Buck Ruxton, with his little daughter.*

Various menial medical jobs followed, but his career never took off. In 1925, he married a Parsee girl from a well-to-do family, quite possibly in an arranged wedding, but they did not get on at all, and Dr Hakim moved out and became a ship's doctor for a while. After receiving a grant from the Bombay Medical Service, he went to further his studies in London, where he attended courses at the University College Hospital under the name of Dr Gabriel Hakim. He then studied in Paris for a while, before going to Edinburgh in 1927, to sit his fellowship exams. The standards upheld by the Edinburgh examiners were a good deal higher than those at Bombay University, however, and Dr Hakim failed his exams on three consecutive occasions. Nevertheless, the kind and forgiving General Medical Council acknowledged Dr Hakim's foreign medical degree, and granted him a license to practice medicine in Britain; an unwise decision indeed, as it would soon turn out: if this sub-continental upstart had instead been given a hard kick in the backside, in the direction of his old haunts back home in India, much mischief would have been averted.

During his residence in Edinburgh, the amorous Dr Hakim had made the acquaintance of the Scottish restaurant waitress Isabella van Ess. The daughter of the deceased mining engineer John Kerr and his wife Elizabeth, she had married, in 1920, the Dutch-American seaman Antonio Cornelis van Ess, of the ship 'Golden State' at Leith. This ill-advised union proved very short-lived, however: after the caddish husband had sailed away, poor Isabella had to return to her dismal chores at the restaurant, and her humble lodgings in Heriot Mount. It is not known whether Dr Hakim ordered a nourishing haggis or some spicy curry when the two first met, but they seem to have fallen in love at first sight. Dr Hakim's swarthy countenance was not a prepossessing sight, and a photograph shows that Isabella was quite plain-looking; yet the passion between this mismatched couple would equal that of Othello and Desdemona, and eventually lead to tragedy.

Since Dr Hakim's grant money had run out, he needed to make a living for himself and his common-law wife Isabella. When he went south of the border to act as locum for a London doctor, he changed his name to Buck Ruxton, for good this time; no forthright friend was at hand to object that although this would have been a good name for an American cowboy, it was something of a ludicrous moniker for a British doctor, particularly one of Indian origins. But Buck worked hard in London and managed to save money, which he made use of to purchase a good medical practice in Lancaster, along with a large terraced town house at No. 2 Dalton Square. One would have thought that the locals in those parts would hardly have appreciated an Indian doctor, but Buck was a personable young man who spoke excellent English; he had a good bedside manner, and seemed to genuinely care for his patients. In spite of his treble humiliation at the hands of the Edinburgh examiners, his medical knowledge was good enough, and he was handy with his surgical knives; during his years in Lancaster, he was never in trouble for any accusation of incompetence, and his practice always had a full complement of patients.

Buck and Isabella soon had three children, but in the 1930s, their relationship steadily deteriorated. Buck was jealous that his wife was 'carrying on' with other men, and Isabella was tearful and hysterical, once attempting suicide, and several times taking the children and returning to Edinburgh, only to come back home when her husband had promised to behave himself. She claimed, quite possibly truly, that Buck had assaulted her more than once, in a furious rage. Buck Ruxton was only just able to keep his practice going, as his family life deteriorated beyond all control.

On September 19 1935, human remains were found near Moffat, Dumfriesshire. Since this was 100 miles north of Lancaster, no person at first linked this sinister finding with the fact that Isabella Ruxton had not been seen for some time, or that the Ruxtons' young nursemaid Mary Rogerson had also disappeared. Ruxton told people that Isabella had gone to Edinburgh, and he tried to fob off Mary's parents by saying that she had gone away to have an abortion in secret, but they did not believe him. It attracted suspicion that Ruxton had removed carpets from his house, and that he had ordered the charwoman who normally cleaned his house to stay away. The body parts from Moffat clearly came from two women, one of them quite young and the other one older. They had been dismembered by an expert hand, like that of a butcher or a doctor: fingers and hands had been cut off, and teeth extracted in order to confound identification via the dental records. The body parts had been wrapped in clothing and newspapers, one of them an edition of the *Sunday Graphic* restricted to the Lancaster and Morecambe area.

Superimposition of photographs of Isabella van Ess and Mary Rogerson onto the skulls of the victims indicated that the remains were from the two missing Lancaster women, and the feet from the body parts exactly fitted their shoes. A pair of child's trousers, in which some body parts had been wrapped, were recognized by a woman as those she had given to one of the Ruxton children. A bedsheet used to wrap up other body parts matched one from Ruxton's house. The carpets and balustrade from the Ruxton house were liberally sprinkled with blood. Witnesses testified as to Ruxton's troubled relationship with his wife, and his previous violence against her. On trial for murder at the Manchester High Court of Justice in March 1936, Ruxton was defended by the eloquent Norman Birkett K.C., but the weight of the forensic evidence against him meant that a guilty verdict could not be avoided. In spite of a petition for clemency, signed by 10 000 people, mainly residents of Lancaster, he was hanged at HM Prison Manchester on May 12 1936.[7] A newspaper published his posthumous confession: he had killed Isabella in a furious rage, and when he realized that Mary Rogerson had seen what he had done, he had murdered her as well.

The Ruxton murder house at No. 2 Dalton Square stood uninhabited for many years, but Lancaster's house of horrors was restored by the town council in the 1980s to be made into offices; it still stands to this day. The police made a curious discovery in the back yard: a deep well covered by a heavy lid; had Ruxton

15. Dr Ruxton's house at No. 2 Dalton Square, Lancaster, which still stands today.

looked closer to home, he would have found an ideal means of hiding the bodies of his victims. The bath from the house, used as evidence during the trial, was made use of as a horse-trough by the mounted division of the Lancashire County Police. The three parentless Ruxton children are believed to have grown up in an orphanage in the Wirral. Ruxton's wax effigy took up residence at Madame Tussaud's, where it remained a popular attraction for many years. Denver's Waxworks in Leith Street, Edinburgh, exhibited Mrs Ruxton's picture, mirrors, hair-brush and table and chairs, purchased for £120, but when the waxworks museum closed down in 1938, the Ruxton memorabilia sold for just £5, a depreciating asset if there ever was one.

★

Robert George Clements was born in Limerick in 1880 and qualified as a M.D. in Belfast in 1904. He got a Diploma in Public Health from Belfast and became a Fellow of the Royal College of Surgeons in 1912. The same year, he married the wealthy heiress Edyth Ann Mercier, whose father died conveniently 18 months later, leaving her £25 000. He had been a patient of Dr Clements, who certified death as being due to cancer. Dr and Mrs Clements were popular members of Belfast society, entertaining lavishly at their large detached house, until the money ran out in 1920. Mrs Clements blamed her hard-spending husband for this state of affairs, but she died not long after, her husband signing the death certificate. After this suspicious business, Dr Clements sold his Belfast practice and moved on to Manchester, where he married yet another heiress who also died mysteriously from 'endocarditis' four years later.

After the demise of the second Mrs Clements, her husband travelled abroad as a ship's doctor for some years, before returning to Manchester in 1927 with a Japanese manservant in tow. The following year, he married an old friend, Katherine Burke, who had known both his previous wives. She was not a particularly wealthy woman, so this time it might well have been a love match. Robert George Clements was a paunchy fellow who looked older than his years, but still he experienced no problems at all in securing a third wife. He worked on as a general practitioner, although his medical knowledge had not benefited from his sojourn in the Orient. To create a niche for himself, he took an interest in herbalism and hydrotherapy, and the administration of medicines via the rear passage instead of the conventional route. In 1933, Dr Clements had had enough of suppositories and anal douches, however; he retired from medical practice and moved south to run a hotel in Bransgore in the New Forest, together with his wife. Since the hotel did not do well, they soon moved to Southport, where they led an active social life for some years, until the money run out. Katherine Clements died in early 1939, from what was supposed to be tuberculosis. A lady doctor friend of hers suspected foul play and pointed out that Dr Clements's two other wives had also died mysteriously, but when she alerted the police, Katherine Clements had just been cremated.

The jolly Robert George Clements carried on his immoral life like if nothing had happened. He soon found himself another prospective wife, or perhaps rather victim: the Southport heiress Amy Victoria Barnett, a woman twenty years his junior. Following a pattern that the reader will now appreciate, her wealthy father, a Liverpool business man, died just a few months later, leaving his daughter a cool £22 000. Dr Clements married Amy Victoria Barnett, and they moved into old man Barnett's luxury flat on the North Promenade in Southport. Since there was by now a war on, the 60-year-old doctor accepted some part-time jobs as a medical officer, but he did not over-exert himself, preferring to spend lavishly to lay waste to yet another fortune coming his way. Dr and Mrs Clements attended plays and musical parties, and led an active social life. But in late 1946, Mrs Clements fell ill with what her husband suspected to be a brain tumour; in February the following year, Dr Clements was telling people that it was only a matter of time before she would die; in May 1947, she entered a nursing home, where she soon expired. But the doctor attending her there suspected that death was due to morphine poisoning and ordered an autopsy to be performed. Unfortunately, the pathologist was a young and gullible doctor, who believed Dr Clements when he said his wife had probably died of myeloid leukaemia, and ordered many of the organs to be destroyed. The nursing home doctor took things further, however: he contacted the coroner and the police, who ordered a second post-mortem performed by a more competent forensic specialist. The police went round to the flat where Dr Clements lived: they found him dead there from a self-administered injection of morphine.[8]

The second post-mortem on Mrs Clements showed evidence that she had died from an injection of morphine. Since the young pathologist who had bungled the first autopsy destroyed himself a few days later, the coroner's inquest would concern two dead doctors and a dead doctor's wife. It ended with the verdict that Mrs Clements had been murdered by Dr Clements, who had then committed suicide. The newspapers had a field-day guessing how many of his previous wives and fathers-in-law the murderous doctor had sent into a premature grave. Throughout his life, they had all died at a most convenient time, allowing the hard-spending doctor to flourish as a result, making good use of the archaic legislation allowing a medical practitioner to issue death certificate in respect of close relatives.

★

Harold Frederick Shipman was born at a council estate in Nottingham on January 14 1946, the second of four children in an undistinguished working-class family. Harold himself had sound cerebral potential, however: he won a scholarship to a good grammar school and entered Leeds University Medical School at the age of 19. He got himself a girlfriend named Primrose, whom he wed in a shotgun marriage after she had become pregnant in some anticontraceptive mishap. The couple soon had two young children. For Shipman there were no carefree days as a medical student, but hard graft and honest toil to support his family. He made good progress through the university curriculum, graduating in 1970 and getting provisionally registered with the General Medical Council. Various junior posts followed, in dreary Northern backwaters, but Harold kept progressing towards his aim in life: to become a general practitioner. He did not have what it takes to go into research, or to aspire to a hospital career, but his aim was to give his family a solid roof over their heads and to start making good money in his medical career. His moment came in March 1974, when he was appointed assistant GP to a large practice in Todmorden. Since his energy, enthusiasm and up-to-date medical knowledge made him popular among the patients, he was promoted to principal GP after just one month.

Dr Shipman took out a mortgage and bought a drab semi-detached house in Todmorden, fully sufficient for his family's needs. He worked extremely hard to make a name for himself as a GP. Unfortunately, he became addicted to the opioid analgesic pethidine, which he injected in increasing amounts to be able to get through his long working days in a pleasant daze of euphoria. Once, he collapsed in the bath and was taken into hospital, but managed to hoodwink the young doctor there that he suffered from epilepsy. But his colleagues discovered that he had faked a large number of prescriptions for pethidine, as well as ordering substantial amounts of the drug on the account of the practice. He was confronted with this blatant misconduct, hounded out of the practice, and forced to enter a rehabilitation clinic as an in-patient. When his case was up before the Halifax Magistrates' Court, Dr Shipman was most contrite and pleaded guilty to forgery of NHS prescriptions, illegal possession of drugs, and obtaining drugs by deception; since the cunning doctor knew how to make a good impression when he made the effort, he was treated very leniently and got off with a fine of just £600. The General Medical Council, which ought to have acted muscularly towards this dangerous, drug-addicted young doctor, just sent him a letter of warning. In 1977, Dr Shipman resurfaced in Hyde, Greater Manchester, having successfully applied for a GP post advertised in the *British Medical Journal*, in the town rendered notorious by the Moors Murderers in the previous decade.

Initially, the slimy Dr Shipman did his best to ingratiate himself with the senior members of the practice, taking on much extra work, becoming popular among his patients, and making himself useful wherever he could. He promised to stay off the pethidine and seemed to have become 'clean', as judged by his prescriptions and the state of the practice's stockpile of this drug. He bought another nondescript semi-detached house and installed his family there, but since the sturdy Primrose had become fed up with cleaning, it soon became very dirty; the unfastidious doctor does not seem to have bothered about this, as long as she kept him well fed with large helpings of nutritious Northern food. With his grey beard, balding head and paunchy belly, he looked a good deal older than his chronological age. As the years went by, he became increasingly angry and irritable, rude to the clerical staff and critical of his fellow doctors. In 1991, he left the practice to set up his own one-doctor surgery in a former shop at No. 21 Market Street, Hyde, taking some of the nursing and clerical staff with him, as well as 3 000 patients.

Dr Shipman's new headquarters at No. 21 Market Street were capacious but looking rather down-at-heel. The unfastidious doctor did not bother much: pleased to be rid of his meddling colleagues, he carried on his solo practice entirely unsupervised. In March 1998, his former GP colleague Dr Linda Reynolds contacted the police after an undertaker had shown her a bundle of cremation forms that Shipman had needed countersigned for his deceased elderly female patients. Regrettably, since the police assigned young and inexperienced officers to the case, they were unable to see through the disguise of the cunning doctor, and no charges were pressed. The next alarm was sounded in August 1998 by the cab driver John Shaw, who had noticed that many of his elderly female clients had died mysteriously in recent times. They all been patients of Dr Shipman! The ultimate cause of the doctor's downfall was the mysterious death of Mrs Kathleen Grundy, a sprightly old lady without any health concerns. She was found dead on June 24; Shipman had been the last person to see her alive, and he signed her death certificate with 'old age' as the cause of death. It also turned out that Mrs Grundy had made a last-minute will, excluding her daughter and her family, and leaving everything to her family doctor. But since the will looked far from authentic, Mrs Grundy's daughter went to the police. An exhumation showed the presence of the potent analgesic diamorphine, used for pain control in terminal cancer patients. Dr Shipman falsified Mrs Grundy's computerized medical records to make it seem if she was a drug addict, but after the police experts had discovered that the records had been tampered with after Mrs Grundy's death, the doctor was arrested. He was found to possess a typewriter of the model used to falsify the will.

The question was of course how many of his patients the murderous Dr Shipman had done away with. The police recognized a lethal pattern of administering high doses of diamorphine, signing the death certificate and falsifying medical records to indicate that the patient had been in very poor health. In October 1999, he went on trial for the murder of his patients, and was found guilty of 15 counts of murder in January 2000, being give the same number of life sentences, with the recommendation that he was never to be released. In the end, he may well have been guilty of 200 or even 250 murders, some of them 'mercy killings' of terminally ill patients, others affecting healthy people with a normal life expectancy. In January 2004, when Shipman was an inmate of Wakefield Prison, he hanged himself from the window bars of his cell using the bedsheets.[9] There was anger among the families of his victims, who felt that he had died without a confession and without providing a motive for his heinous acts, but the irrepressible *Sun* newspaper openly exulted that he was dead, with the headline 'Ship! Ship! Hooray!' In 2005, when I went to deliver a lecture at the Royal Society of Medicine in London, I met two old doctors who had known Shipman. He had been much disliked among his colleagues, particular after his departure from the practice in Hyde, taking his patients with him. They both took it for granted, having heard persistent rumours in the Northern medical circles, that his suicide had been facilitated by the prison officers, who had thought it no great loss if the murderous doctor ended up in a coffin sooner rather than later.

So what made Dr Shipman into the murderous monster he became; what fiend from Hell was lurking behind the mask of Dr Jekyll of Hyde? His mother died from cancer when he was a youngster, being treated with high doses of morphine, but although the cod psychologists have pointed out the injurious effects this might have to his dormant intellect, many people experience such tragedies without developing into serial killers. He led a generally humdrum and disappointing life, living in squalid conditions and having few interests apart from medicine. Perhaps he began his career facilitating the deaths of some terminally ill patients by withdrawing treatment, going on to actively killing them with an overdose of morphine, and ending up killing also the healthy and fit among his elderly patients, just because he could. His lack of both religion and spirituality must have meant that he viewed diseased human beings just as waste to be disposed of. As for Dr Shipman's old surgery at No. 21 Market Street, Hyde, it closed down in 2002, the remaining patients being transferred to another health centre. In 2006, it was refitted as a shop, and it is today the 'Eat At 21' Indian restaurant.

XIV.

CONCLUDING REMARKS

To be able to undertake a review of murderous doctors in Britain, it is of course important first to define who qualifies as a medical practitioner. In this book, I have decided to leave out the serial poisoner Severin Klosowski, otherwise known as George Chapman, since he possessed only a rudimentary education as a barber-surgeon in Poland, and never practiced in either Britain or the United States.[1] It is true that Dr Crippen did not have a license to practice in Britain, but he at least had a tolerably good American medical degree, and had practiced there for some years. Nor is there room for Dr Thomas Smethurst, although he was a bona fide doctor, since there is evidence that his alleged victim in fact died from inflammatory bowel disease, and Smethurst was acquitted after a thorough review of the case by a medical expert.[2]

This leaves us with a total of eight murderous medical miscreants, from Palmer to Shipman. None of them was a particularly good or distinguished doctor, although it speaks in Dr Pritchard's favour that he wrote at least one book and a number of articles in medical journals. Pritchard, Ruxton, Clements and Shipman were all hard-working GPs, whose medical knowledge was sufficient to keep the negligence lawyer away. Palmer does not appear to have taken his medical career very seriously, although he was never a dangerous or grossly incompetent doctor. Lamson was very successful as a military surgeon, but he found general practice pointless and dull; although his progressive addiction to morphine made him a dangerous doctor indeed, all his Bournemouth patients seem to have survived his ministrations. Just like Lamson, Cream received a good medical education, but his career never took off and he ended up as a mere abortionist, before his Chicago conviction for murder ended his medical career, for good. Nor can Crippen be said to have been a particularly good doctor: his medical degree was a low-quality one and he belonged to the grey-zone between 'doctor' and 'quack' that existed in America in those days, finally ending up as a patent medicine salesman.

Venenation has been the modus operandi of seven out of eight of the deadly doctors, Ruxton being the odd man out, but then this wife-beating cad seems to have been a desperate and excitable character, with a low level of self-control and a strong predilection for domestic violence. Palmer made use of strychnine and antimony, Pritchard dosed his victims with antimony, Cream used strychnine, Crippen hyoscine, and Clements and Shipman both morphine. Palmer was an appalling case study of alcoholism and gambling addiction, whose tally of victims may well have been a considerable one, given how many people who had died mysteriously in his immediate surroundings. The registration of the sale of poisons, which would lead to the downfall of Pritchard and Lamson, was quite deficient in his days. As shown by Palmer, Pritchard and Clements, a murderous doctor can be a formidable criminal: cold and calculating, yet universally trusted, and able to sign the death certificates of his victims himself. For him, one victim is not enough, and murder soon becomes a way of getting money and achieve the elimination of various undesirable people. Cream was an even more horrible case study of alcoholism, drug abuse, perversion and pure evil. Crippen was the sole 'good guy' among the eight medical miscreants, an ordinary man driven to desperation by his overbearing wife, and his passion for Ethel Le Neve. As for that monster Shipman, he will fortunately remain a *unicum* when it comes to medical mass slaughter.

Comparing his murderous career with those of the prolific killers Palmer and Pritchard, it seems likely that Dr Lamson murdered Hubert William John as well, and got away with it. As a military surgeon, he had seen that life was cheap, with the wounded soldiers dying like flies; now both Hubert and Percy were invalids, crippled by tuberculosis and scoliosis, worthless and parasitic existences whose sufferings should be put an end to, he must have reasoned, like hastening the death of a badly mutilated soldier. His wife would be a useful tool to do some money-laundering after her brothers had been decimated, with the Doctor flourishing briefly as a result. Perhaps the greatest mystery in the Lamson case is why he did not wait until he had Percy under his influence at the Chichester hotel, where the invalid could be given some 'medicine' with complete security, before Lamson signed the death certificate himself. There may well be some truth in the story that Lamson thought the aconitine was an untraceable poison, but nevertheless, he had taken one risk too many and this would lead to his downfall. Through his escalating morphine abuse, George Henry Lamson had created a fearsome Golem in his own image, a perfectly amoral creature capable of killing with coolness and premeditation; this once brave and promising young doctor had become both Dr Jekyll and Mr Hyde, both Frankenstein and murderous Monster, as he sped towards his doom on a Highway to Hell.

FOOTNOTES

PREFACE

1. Lindsay Siviter and the late Robert Linford are thanked for additional research, Nicholas Connell for a critical reading of part of the manuscript, and Stewart McLaughlin for showing me Wandsworth Prison and its Museum.

CHAPTER I
1. W.J. Lamson, *Descendants of William Lamson of Ipswich, Mass. 1634-1917* (New York 1917).
2. *Morning Chronicle* Aug 16 1858.
3. On the Paris activities of the Rev. Mr Lamson, see C. Allen, *The History of the American Pro-Cathedral, Church of the Holy Trinity. Paris (1815-1980)* (Bloomington IN 2012), pp. 35-190.
4. *Church Journal* Oct 5 and 12 1864.
5. *Times* May 1 1865.
6. *Times* Oct 25 1870. On the Franco-Prussian war and its sequel, see A. Horne, *The Fall of Paris* (London 1965).
7. *Bradford Observer* April 25 1871; Allen, p. 171.
8. Quoted by Allen, pp. 165-6.
9. On the American Ambulance, see T.W. Evans, *History of the American Ambulance* (London 1873) and the articles by R. Keeler (*Lippincott's Magazine* 12 [1873], 84-92) and G. Seltzer (*Madison Historical Review* 6 [2009], 1-20).
10. Quoted by Allen, pp. 171-2.

CHAPTER II

1. There is still a Sydney Lodge standing at Bath Road, Ventnor, although it has been subdivided into flats.
2. Allen, p. 164.
3. Quoted by Allen, p. 177.
4. Allen, pp 178-80.
5. *Penny Illustrated Paper* March 25 1882, *York Herald* March 25 1882. A mystification is added by the fact that the Wellcome Collection holds (A651599) what is purported to be Dr Lamson's diary for 1874, along with a *bona fide* newspaper cutting about the case. Since the 1970s, these items have been deposited at the stores of the Science Museum at Blythe House, West Kensington, along with a collection of medical instruments. It is the London 'Letts's Pocket Diary and an Almanac for 1874', marked 'G.H.L.' but not by the Doctor's hand. It contains the address of a certain Mr J. Phillips, of No. 22 Elgin Crescent, Notting Hill, and another address in 'Marine Parade'. But since Dr Lamson was in the United States during all of 1874, he hardly had any need to collect London addresses; the pocket diary is likely to have belonged to another 'G.H.L.' who was in London at the time. There is no clue forthcoming why this diary was linked with Lamson in the first place.
6. *Hampshire Telegraph* Aug 10 1872.
7. *Leeds Mercury* Oct 10 1872.
8. *Morning Post* April 19 1873.
9. *Pall Mall Gazette* April 28 1873.
10. *Dundee Courier* July 11 1873.
11. *Hampshire Advertiser* Aug 5 1874.
12. J.L. Farley, *The League in Aid of the Christians of Turkey* (London 1878).
13. On the Balkan crisis, see W.G. Wirthwein, *Britain and the Balkan Crisis 1875-1878* (New York 1966) and D. Harris, *A*

Diplomatic History of the Balkan Crisis of 1875-1878 (New York 1969).
14. NA J 90/1614.
15. *Jackson's Oxford Journal* Nov 18 1876.
16. NA J 90/1614.
17. *New York Times* Dec 22 1876.
18. NA J 90/1614.
19. *Daily News* Aug 24 1877.
20. *Daily News* Oct 10 1877.
21. *Daily News* Oct 19 1877.
22. *Daily News* Nov 17 1877.
23. *Standard* Nov 5 1877.
24. J.L. Farley, *The League in Aid of the Christians of Turkey* (London 1878), p. 43.
25. *Daily News* Dec 3 1877.
26. *Dundee Courier* March 17 1882.

CHAPTER III

1. *Lancet* i [1878], 735. The relevant entry in the Register of Licentiates is dated May 7 1878; it does not provide Lamson's address in Edinburgh, merely his place of birth as New York.
2. On Horse Grove, see C. Pullein, *Rotherfield* (Tunbridge Wells 1928), pp. 316-22.
3. *British Medical Journal* ii [1878], 607. The marriage was also announced in the *Pall Mall Gazette* Oct 24 1878 and in the *Hampshire Telegraph* Oct 26 1878.
4. NA C 16/579/1/J88.
5. H.L. Adam, *The Trial of George Henry Lamson* (Notable British Trials, London 1912), p. 14.
6. *Standard* Aug 20 1879; the birth was also announced in the *Pall Mall Gazette* Aug 19 1879.

7. *Kent & Sussex Courier* Dec 31 2010.
8. Adam, p. 33.
9. Allen, pp 185-6.
10. *Bournemouth Echo* Aug 31 2010.
11. Adam, p. 188; NA HO 144/90/A11385/67.
12. *Hampshire Telegraph* Oct 9 1880.
13. NA CRIM 1/13/3/136.
14. *Lancet* i [1882], 281. The original letters are at the archives of the Royal College of Physicians of Edinburgh, FEL/3/88.
15. NA HO 144/90/A11385/67.
16. NA HO 144/90/A11385/115; *Bristol Mercury* April 20 1882; Adam, p. 33. Radclyffe Radclyffe-Hall married the American widow Mary Jane Sager in 1878, but they divorced in 1882. Their surviving daughter was the notorious Marguerite Antonia Radclyffe-Hall, author of the *Well of Loneliness* and other works.
17. Adam, pp. 118-20.

CHAPTER IV

1. NA HO 144/90/A11385/196-7; Adam, p. 119.
2. Adam, pp. 208-9.
3. Adam, pp. 201-4.
4. Adam, p. 120.
5. Adam, p. 204.
6. Adam, pp. 206-8.
7. NA CRIM 1/13/3/141-5.
8. Adam, pp. 197-8.
9. Adam, pp. 92-3, 116-7; NA CRIM 1/13/3.
10. Adam, p. 209.
11. Adam, pp. 85-90.
12. NA CRIM 1/13/3/131-5.

13. NA CRIM 1/13/3/186-7
14. NA CRIM 1/13/3/188-9.
15. On this disgraceful episode, see Adam, pp. 120-1.
16. NA CRIM 1/13/3/194.
17. Adam, pp. 122-4; NA CRIM 1/13/3. Tulloch is likely to have been born in Livingston, West Lothian, in 1856.
18. Adam, pp. 122-3.

CHAPTER V

1. The best account of Mr Bedbrooks's evidence is in NA CRIM 1/13/3; see also Adam, pp. 49-57.
2. Adam, p. 129.
3. The evidence of the doctors is in NA CRIM 1/13/3; see also Adam, pp. 68-76.
4. Adam, pp. 76-9.
5. *Daily News* Dec 5 1881.
6. *Pall Mall Gazette* Dec 5 1881.
7. *Standard* Dec 5 1881.
8. Adam, pp. 70-1.
9. On the opening of the inquest, see *Pall Mall Gazette* Dec 7 1881 and *Standard* Dec 7 1881.
10. *Standard* Dec 9 1881, *Reynolds's Newspaper* Dec 11 1881.
11. *Leeds Mercury* Dec 7 1881.
12. *Standard* Dec 6 1881, *Birmingham Daily Post* Dec 6 1881.
13. Quoted in the *Huddersfield Daily Chronicle* Dec 7 1881 and *Glasgow Herald* Dec 7 1881.
14. *Pall Mall Gazette* Dec 8 1881.

CHAPTER VI

1. NA HO 144/90/A11385/6.
2. Adam, p. 127.
3. Adam, pp. 127-9.
4. *Daily News* Dec 9 1881.
5. *Birmingham Daily Post* Dec 9 1881. G. St Aubyn, *Infamous Victorians* (London 1971), p. 165, gives a description of Dr Lamson 'in his threadbare frockcoat' that appears to be based on imagination alone.
6. *Times* Dec 9 1881, *Daily News* Dec 9 1881, *Northern Echo* Dec 9 1881.
7. *Western Mail* Dec 9 1881.
8. *Daily News* Dec 10 1881.
9. *Pall Mall Gazette* Dec 16 1881.
10. *Morning Post* Dec 17 1881, *Reynolds's Newspaper* Dec 18 1881.
11. M. Williams, *Leaves of a Life* (London 1890).
12. J. Bondeson, *Rivals of the Ripper* (Stroud 2016), pp. 64-7.
13. *Daily News* Dec 21 1881, *Morning Post* Dec 21 1881.
14. *Daily News* Dec 23 1881.
15. *Morning Post* Dec 23 1881, *Reynolds's Newspaper* Dec 25 1881.
16. *Times* Dec 24 1881.
17. *Daily News* Dec 30 1881, *Morning Post* Dec 30 1881.

CHAPTER VII

1. *Pall Mall Gazette* Dec 30 1881.
2. Quoted in the *Dundee Courier* Jan 4 1882.
3. *Morning Post* Dec 31 1881, *Lloyd's Weekly Newspaper* Jan 1 1882, *Reynolds's Newspaper* Jan 1 1882.
4. *Morning Post* Dec 31 1881.
5. The letters are in *Times* Jan 3 1882 and *Daily News* Jan 3

1882; the session was also covered by *Standard* Jan 3 1882 and *Morning Post* Jan 3 1882.
6. *Times* Jan 7 1882, *Daily News* Jan 7 1882, *Morning Post* Jan 7 1882.
7. *Sheffield and Rotherham Independent* Feb 21 1883.
8. *Nottinghamshire Guardian* Feb 23 1883.
9. *North-Eastern Daily Gazette* March 2 1883, *Derby Daily Telegraph* April 18 1883.

CHAPTER VIII

1. The trial is ably described by Adam; see also OldBaileyOnline as well as *Morning Post* and *Daily News* for March 10-14 1882.

CHAPTER IX

1. *Pall Mall Gazette* March 15 and 16 1882.
2. *Referee* March 19 1882.
3. Leaked to the *Daily News* March 17 1882.
4. *Times* March 17 1882.
5. *Daily News* March 18 1882.
6. *Times* March 21 1882.
7. *Pall Mall Gazette* March 23 1882.
8. *Pall Mall Gazette* March 24 1882.
9. The originals can be read in NA 144/90/A11385/37; there is a summary of some of them in Adam, pp. 192-209.
10. *Dundee Courier* March 18 1882.
11. Radclyffe Radclyffe-Hall married Mary Jane Sager in 1878, but she divorced him on grounds of cruelty in 1882, after she had given birth to their daughter Marguerite. He died

in 1907 aged just 52, see M. Baker, *Our Three Selves* (London 1985), pp. 9-13.
12. NA HO 144/90/A11385/112.
13. The letters are in NA HO 144/90/A11385/14, 16, 19, 40, 49, 54, 66, 76, 80 and 141.
14. On the case of Dr Thomas Smethurst, convicted of murdering his mistress in 1859 but given a free pardon after a medical expert had examined the case, see J. Bondeson, *Murder Houses of South London* (Leicester 2015), pp. 180-6.
15. NA HO 144/90/A11385/14 and 76. Edward Henry Stuart Bligh, Lord Clifton (1851-1900) was the son of the Earl of Darnley. Described as a volatile character, he was a useful cricketer as a young man, playing for Eton and Kent.
16. NA HO 144/90/A11385/19 and 49. Dr Henry Arthur Allbutt was a controversial Leeds doctor, a member of the Malthusian League and an advocate of birth control; he was the author of *The Wife's Handbook* and *Every Mother's Handbook*. In 1887, he was struck off the Medical Register.
17. *Pall Mall Gazette* March 27 1882.
18. *Pall Mall Gazette* March 28 1882, *Morning Post* March 28 1882, *Standard* March 29 1882.
19. NA HO 144/90/A11385/73-74; *Pall Mall Gazette* March 31 1882.
20. NA HO 144/90/A11385/37; *Times* April 3 1882, *Pall Mall Gazette* April 3 1882.
21. *Hansard* 268 [1882] (April 3), 551-3.
22. *Pall Mall Gazette* April 3 1882.
23. *Moonshine* April 8 1882.
24. *Moonshine* March 25 1882.
25. *Sporting Times* April 22 1882.
26. *Funny Folks* April 29 1882.
27. *Times* April 6 1882; also published in the *Standard* of April 6 1882 and *Lloyd's Weekly Newspaper* of April 9 1882, and quoted by many other newspapers.

28. *Morning Post* April 14 1882, *Standard* April 14 1882. US President James Abram Garfield, murdered by the assassin Guiteau in 1881, was the predecessor of Chester Arthur. The affidavits of Watson and Phillips are in NA HO 144/90/A11385/13 and 115.
29. *Pall Mall Gazette* April 17 1882.
30. *Referee* April 9 1882.
31. NA HO 144/90/A11385/112.
32. NA HO 144/90/A11385/77 and 112. Most, but not all, of the US affidavits are abstracted by Adam; see also *Daily News* April 15 and 18, *Times* April 18 and 19 1882.
33. NA HO 144/90/A11385/42 and 89.
34. NA HO 144/90/A11385/112.
35. NA HO 144/90/A11385/95.
36. NA HO 144/90/A11385/112; *Times* April 18 1882.
37. NA HO 144/90/A11385/79.
38. NA HO 144/90/A11385/112.
39. *Referee* April 16 1882.
40. *Pall Mall Gazette* April 17 1882.
41. Quoted in the *Pall Mall Gazette* April 20 1882.
42. *Referee* April 23 1882.
43. *Morning Post* April 26 and 27 1882.
44. *Pall Mall Gazette* April 27 1882.
45. Published in the *Daily News*, April 27 1882.

CHAPTER X

1. *Birmingham Daily Press* April 28 1882, *Leeds Mercury* April 28 1882. Nothing is known about the activities of Mrs Julia Lamson after this date.
2. Published in the *Times* April 28 1882.
3. *Daily Telegraph* April 29 1882.

4. There are accounts of the execution of Lamson in the *Times* April 29 1882, *Pall Mall Gazette* April 28 1882 and *Birmingham Daily Press* April 29 1882; the fullest is in the *Daily Telegraph* April 29 1882. Dr Lamson's death cell is today a prison office; the execution shed has long since been demolished; a small garden marks the place of the unmarked graves of the prisoners executed at Wandsworth Prison, with an ornamental tree planted near the Doctor's final place of rest.
5. *Times* April 28 1882 and other newspapers.
6. NA HO 144/90/A11385/133.
7. *Referee* April 30 1882.
8. *Standard* May 1 and 30 1882, *Reynolds's Newspaper* May 7 1882, *Morning Post* May 30 1882.
9. *Nottingham Evening Post* June 10 1882.
10. *Ipswich Journal* June 20 1882.
11. *Bell's Life in London* Jan 27 1883, *Edinburgh Evening News* March 26 1883.
12. *Chambers' Journal* April 25 1885.
13. *Evening Standard* Sept 2 1889.
14. *Nottingham Evening Post* May 26 1924.

CHAPTER XI

1. *Morning Post* Dec 31 1881.
2. *Liverpool Mercury* March 17 1882.
3. M. Williams, *Leaves of a Life* (London 1890), p. 300.
4. *Morning Post* April 28 1882.
5. NA HO 144/90/A11385/133. A conspiracy theorist would of course suggest that Montagu Williams was right, and that to hide the fact that Dr Lamson was a double murderer, a story was leaked to the newspapers that Lamson had confessed but denied murdering Hubert, before a written confession was falsified.

6. T.Y.K. Chan (*Clinical Toxicology* 47 [2009], 279-85).
7. P. Macinnis, *Poisons* (London 2005), pp. 25-6.
8. Reviews on aconitine include those by Y. Fujita *et al.* (*Journal of Analytical Toxicology* 31 [2007], 132-7) and T.Y.K. Chan (*Clinical Toxicology* 47 [2009], 279-85).
9. T.Y.K. Chan (*Clinical Toxicology* 47 [2009], 279-85).
10. F.S. Fiddes (*British Medical Journal* ii [1958], 779-80).
11. N. Yoshioka *et al.* (*Forensic Medicine International* 81 [1996], 117-23).
12. Quoted by T.Y.K. Chan (*Clinical Toxicology* 47 [2009], 279-85).
13. H. Niinuma *et al.* (*Internet Journal of Emergency and Intensive Care Medicine* 6(2), 2003.
14. *Edmonton Journal* Aug 7 2004, R. Pullela *et al.* (*Journal of Forensic Science* 53 [2008], 491-4).
15. *Daily Mail* Jan 8 and Feb 11 2010, *BBC News* Feb 10 and 11 2010.
16. Adam, p. 18.
17. Adam, pp. 27-8.
18. *Observer* April 30 1882.
19. *Referee* April 30 1882.
20. *British Medical Journal* i [1882], 584-6.
21. M. Whittington-Egan, *The Execution of Mary Ansell* (London 2017).
22. J. Bondeson, *Victorian Murders* (Stroud 2017), pp. 52-7, and its references.
23. J. Bondeson, *Murder Houses of Greater London* (Leicester 2015), pp. 242-6, and its references.
24. See the articles by E. Lomax (*Bulletin of the History of Medicine* 47 [1973], 167-76), V. Berridge (*Victorian Studies* 21 [1978], 437-61) and D. Peters (*Journal of the History of Medicine and Allied Sciences* 46 [1981], 455-88).
25. J. Lewy (*War in History* 21 [2013], 102-19).
26. H. Obersteiner (*Brain* 2 [1879-80], 449-65).

27. B. Milligan (*Victorian Literature and Culture* 33 [2005], 541-53).

CHAPTER XII

1. W. Wood, *Survivors' Tales of Famous Crimes* (London 1916), pp. 260-1.
2. C. Kingston, *A Gallery of Rogues* (London 1924), pp. 67-9.
3. *Hastings and St Leonards Observer* Dec 31 1910.
4. *New York Daily Tribune* June 1 1907.
5. *Living Church Annual*, 1910, p. 144.
6. *Standard* Dec 15 1898, *Morning Post* Dec 15 1898, C. Kingston, *A Gallery of Rogues* (London 1924), pp. 68-9.
7. *Northern Daily Mail* Oct 13 1928.
8. *Dundee Evening Telegraph* Aug 23 1921.
9. *Famous Crimes Past & Present* [1904]: 4(49), 218-22 and 4(50), 248-52.
10. Emails from H. Herrington, London Borough of Merton.
11. C. Pullein, *Rotherfield* (Tunbridge Wells 1928), pp. 316-22.
12. Bournemouth Library, 'Local Biography', Vol. 19; *Bournemouth Echo* Aug 31 2010.
13. R. Harris (Ed.), *The Reminscences of Sir Henry Hawkins, Baron Brampton*, 2 vols (London 1904).
14. The account of the Lamson trial is in M. Williams, *Leaves of a Life* (London 1890), pp. 294-300; he also published *Later Leaves* (London 1891) and *Round London* (London 1892). There were obituaries in the *Illustrated London News* Dec 31 1892 and in the *British Medical Journal* ii [1892], 1440.
15. His biography by E. Bowen-Rowlands, *Seventy-Two Years at the Bar* (London 1924), has an account of the Lamson case on pp. 186-9.

CHAPTER XIII

1. On Dr Palmer, see G.H. Knott (Ed.), *Trial of William Palmer* (London 1912), G. Fletcher, *The Life and Career of Dr William Palmer of Rugeley* (London 1925), D. Barker, *Palmer the Rugeley Poisoner* (London 1935), D. Lewis, *The Rugeley Poisoner* (Stafford 2003) and S. Bates, *The Poisoner* (London 2014).
2. On Dr Pritchard, see W. Roughead (Ed.), *Trial of Dr Pritchard* (Glasgow 1906) and R. Gilbank, *The Prettiest Liar* (Hull 2012); also the articles by G.H. Edington (*Glasgow Medical Journal* Feb 1912, 104-9) and S.T. Green & F.A.M. Green (*Scottish Medical Journal* 31 [1986], 256-60).
3. The two main books on Dr Cream are W.T. Shore, *Trial of Neill Cream* (London 1923) and A. McLaren, *A Prescription for Murder* (Chicago 1993); see also the articles by J. Bloomfield (*Criminologist* 15 [1991], 224-44 and *Ripper Notes* 23 [2005], 50-8) and P.J. Reiter (*College Literature* 35 [2008], 57-90).
4. *Pall Mall Gazette* Oct 22 1892.
5. There are many books about Dr Crippen, among them F. Young (Ed.), *The Trial of Hawley Harvey Crippen* (Edinburgh 1933), M. Constantine Quinn, *Doctor Crippen* (London 1935), T. Cullen, *Crippen: The Mild Murderer* (London 1977), D.J. Smith, *Supper with the Crippens* (London 2005), and N. Connell, *Doctor Crippen* (Stroud 2013), and the article by A. Samuels (*Medicine, Science and the Law* 50 [2010], 57-9).
6. D.R. Foran *et al.* (*Journal of Forensic Sciences* 56 [2011], 233-40); N. Connell, *Doctor Crippen* (Stroud 2013), pp. 171-85.
7. On the Ruxton case, see R.H. Blundell & G.H. Wilson (Eds.), *Trial of Buck Ruxton* (London 1950) and *Murder Casebook*, Volume 4, Issue 48, 1990.
8. On Dr Clements, see J. Camp, *One Hundred Years of Medical Murder* (London 1982), pp. 176-91 and G. Wright, *Foul Deeds and Suspicious Deaths around Southport* (Barnsley 2008), pp. 6-34.

9. On Dr Shipman, see W. Clarkson, *The Good Doctor* (London 2001) and C. Peters, *Harold Shipman* (London 2005); a particularly good account is that by R. Whittington-Egan, *Tales from the Dead-House* (Stroud 2016), pp. 7-84. See also the articles by H.G. Kinnell (*British Medical Journal* 321 [2000], 1594-7) and C. Gilleard (*Journal of Aging Studies* 22 [2008], 88-95), as well as the *Daily Mirror* for Feb 1 2000.

CHAPTER XIV

1. J. Bondeson, *Murder Houses of South London* (Leicester 2015), pp. 25-30 and its references.
2. J. Bondeson, *Murder Houses of South London* (Leicester 2015), pp. 180-6.

A NOTE ON SOURCES

There was a contemporary pamphlet about *The Life and Trial of Dr Lamson*, published on April 5 1882 by G. Purkess, the proprietor of the *Illustrated Police News*, and sold for a penny at his office in 286 Strand; it promised to provide interesting particulars never before published, and was illustrated with portraits and views. It was advertised in the *Illustrated Police News* of March 25 and April 1 1882, when Lamson was awaiting execution. Not a single copy of this rare pamphlet is kept in any library today, however, nor have I ever seen it advertised for sale on the Internet. The earliest full-length book on the Lamson case is H.L. Adam, *The Trial of George Henry Lamson* (Notable British Trials, London 1912). The trial is competently described, using the Old Bailey Sessions Papers, with some useful appendices from the *Daily Telegraph*.

Hargrave Lee Adam (1867-1946) was a prominent true crime writer of his day, with excellent police contacts, who published the *Police Encyclopaedia* in eight volumes and sixteen other old crime books; on his biography, see N. Connell (*New Independent Review* 3 [2012], 1-24). I have elsewhere (*Rivals of the Ripper* (Stroud 2016), pp. 95-6, 151, 323) pointed out that Adam was sometimes careless and lacking in judgment, and I would not be disposed to agree with him that Percy Malcolm John was poisoned via the Dundee cake. Nor is his introduction to the trial report always factually reliable: he calls Percy John's brother Hubert William 'Herbert' and puts Nelson's Hotel in 'Portland Road' instead of in Great Portland Street. The trial of George Henry Lamson is available on OldBaileyOnline, and it generally agrees well with the trial report given by Hargrave Adam. The second major study on the Lamson case is G. St Aubyn, *Infamous Victorians* (London 1971), pp. 155-236. The Hon. Giles St Aubyn (1925-2015), the son of Lord St Levan, read history at Trinity College, Oxford, and became an Eton master, spending many years as an educationalist as well as writing twelve books on popular history; his obituary is in the *Times* of July 15 2015. His book is not annotated, and imagination is sometimes made use of where facts are scarce, leading to several errors being introduced. Due to the inherent unreliability of this book, and its failure to add anything new or interesting to Adam's account, it has been made little use of in my account of the case. Neither Adam nor St Aubyn appears to have consulted the voluminous police and Home Office files on the Lamson case: NA CRIM 1/13/3 and HO 144/90/A11385. There are many shorter accounts of the Lamson case, listed here in chronological order: G.R. Sims, *The Death Gamble* (London 1909), pp. 147-62, W. Wood, *Survivors' Tales of Famous Crimes* (London 1916), pp. 246-61, H. Eaton, *Famous Poison Trials* (London 1923), pp. 13-53, E. Bowen-Rowlands, *Seventy-two Years at the Bar* (London 1924), pp. 186-9, C. Kingston, *A Gallery of Rogues* (London 1924), pp. 67-9, L.A. Perry, *Some Famous Medical*

Trials (New York 1928), pp. 88-103, R. Furneaux, *The Medical Murderer* (London 1957), pp. 42-7, J. Rowland, *Poisoner in the Dock* (London 1960), pp. 15-29, M. Hardwick, *Doctors on Trial* (London 1961), pp. 79-114, S. Dewes, *Doctors of Murder* (London 1962), pp. 85-103, S.M. Rabson (*Journal of the American Medical Association* 216 [1971], 121-4), J. Camp, *One Hundred Years of Medical Murder* (London 1982), pp. 69-94, A.W. Moss (*Master Detective* May 2004, 37-42) and L. Stratmann, *Greater London Murders* (Stroud 2010), pp. 197-204, and *The Secret Poisoner* (New Haven CT 2016), pp. 238-45. Newspaper accounts of Dr Lamson's career include *Wanganui Chronicle* Aug 21 1919, *Bath Chronicle* March 12 1921, *Aberdeen Evening Express* Jan 24 1958, *Bournemouth Echo* June 5 1973 and Aug 31 2010, and *Kent & Sussex Courier* Dec 31 2010.

Two key works are referred to by short title, namely H.L. Adam, *The Trial of George Henry Lamson* (Notable British Trials, London 1912) and C. Allen, *The History of the American Pro-Cathedral, Church of the Holy Trinity. Paris (1815-1980)* (Bloomington IN 2012).

A NOTE ON LAMSONIAN ICONOGRAPHY

There was definitely at least one CDV portrait of Dr Lamson. One of these cards was kept at the Black Museum for a while and shown to visitors in the 1880s, but it is today lost, presumably stolen by one of the museum custodians, or perhaps by some thieving visitor. The article by Moss in the *Master Detective* of May 2004 has an illustration that might well have come from a CDV, albeit very badly reproduced; since that unsophisticated magazine does not provide sources for its illustrations, and since its editor has no memory of events back in 2004, we will never know for sure. There were many newspaper and magazine images of Lamson and the other main players in the case, all of them reproduced in this book. Hargrave Adam managed to unearth a good likeness of Dr Lamson "from a drawing by P.B. Whelpley.". It turns out that the artist Philip Breed Whelpley was born in 1870, so he could not have been very old when he executed this drawing. He served as a Lieutenant in the US Naval Reserve Force during the Great War and was alive as late as 1944.

For exclusive discounts on Matador titles,
sign up to our occasional newsletter at
troubador.co.uk/bookshop

www.ingramcontent.com/pod-product-compliance
Lightning Source LLC
LaVergne TN
LVHW010313070526
838199LV00065B/5548